D0597338

Other books by Eddie Campbell

Alec: The King Canute Crowd

From Hell (with Alan Moore)

The Birth Caul (with Alan Moore)

In preparation

After the Snooter

Snakes and Ladders (with Alan Moore)

eddie campbell

alec *how to be an artist*

eddie campbell comics
2001

ALEC: HOW TO BE AN ARTIST
First printing March 2001
Published by Eddie Campbell Comics
PO Box 230, Paddington Q 4064, Australia.
Internet: http://www.eddiecampbellcomics.com
email: eddie@eddiecampbellcomics.com

Book designed by Michael Evans.
PRINTED IN CANADA.
Available in the US from: Chris Staros,
Top Shelf Productions, PO Box 1282, Marietta GA 30061-1282.
Internet: http://www.topshelfcomix.com
ISBN 0 9577896 3 7

PUBLISHING HISTORY

How to be an artist originally appeared in serial form from 1997 to 2000 in issues 1 to 14 of **Dee Vee** and one episode appeared in **The Staros Report 1997**. The book has been considerably expanded and revised for this edition.

Foreword

In this book, I started out to create something from my experiences in trying to make a living as an artist; to turn them into lessons by distilling them into recognisable formulæ ('If you do *a* then *b* will follow.' Oh, the daring literary conceit!). I wanted to recreate the types of artistic personalities that one is sure to encounter once set out upon this road. However, I then overstepped my preset boundary and it became an account of the rise and fall of what has become known as the graphic novel. This bigger task required me to relate the doings of particular personalities. I carefully weighed up the question of whether to name names and decided that the work would be a much lesser thing if I didn't. The *Alec* persona has been carried over from my earlier books (*The King Canute Crowd, Graffiti Kitchen*) for the reason that I found it easier to talk to myself in the future tense that way. Otherwise I have attempted to make the tale an account of a phase of popular art, giving sample reproductions in the way that books of this kind normally do. If you don't care for history, then just pretend that I made it all up. Either way you'll probably end up gasping in disbelief.

Eddie Campbell
February 2001

Well, we've had the artistic adventure; now let's have a real one. We'll rob a train and ride like blazes for the border.

Noel Sickles 1934

For my art buddies Dakin and Elliott.

(Dakes and me on the back cover, photo by Elliott)

How to successfully be an ARTIST (not to be confused with 'becoming a successful artist')

FIRST, you must make your bargain with FATE

I will Cherish not material security but will squander it all in the search for wisdom.

Furthermore, I will only lie in the service of TRUTH

Then you must get the most dead-end job you can find, one that does not require intelligence, because you will need to deploy that elsewhere.

You must put yourself through an informal course of learning everything there is to learn.

This is not to be confused with learning everything you need to know. You could easily go to college for that.

This will take the rest of eternity.

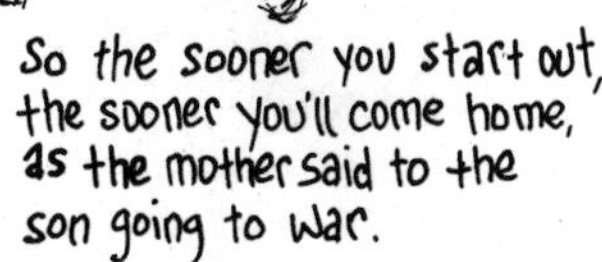

So the sooner you start out, the sooner you'll come home, as the mother said to the son going to war.

Once you have made your decision you may wait a while for the change to fall upon you from heaven.

However, your cue to step out onto the stage will be clear and precise. One day the pointless job will finish. The factory will close down

From that moment you may confidently describe yourself as an ARTIST Do not be deterred.

you. mean an unemployed one!

At your own small expense put your work where it will be seen and continue to be seen. It's the age of the photocopier. Quality reproduction is available to all.

In direct consequence, one day a letter will arrive in the mail.

Alec MacCarry
Westcliff Parade
Southend-on-Sea
Essex

This will be your communication from The Man at the Crossroads.

He will not be a practitioner, but an 'amateur'. If you expected someone experienced and with a sphere of influence, you obviously don't know how these things work. If you get someone like that, you can't be very deep.

He need not be aware that FATE has already assigned him a title, nor need you for that matter. Like yourself he has been freed up for his purpose. That's all that matters.

He will be the purest, most fresh-faced wee fellow you have ever met. His ingenuous enthusiasm will beam from his cheery countenance.

The man at the Crossroads will open the next door.

You see, I run a table at the bi-monthly comic marts in Westminster. I invite anybody to put their homemade comic on it, all takings to the producer.

You will undoubtedly ask what he gets out of it. such cynicism should be considered a lapse of faith in the bargain you made with FATE. You will only be permitted three such lapses.

Furthermore, you'll meet other artists whom you see to be on a similar mission of TRUTH, and you'll tell them so.

Hey, can you do me a two pager for my comic, Phil?
Yeh, great! can you do me one?

Once started, things will move faster than you expected. your little show will get a write-up in the hip music press.

Page 32 — New Musical Express 29th May, 1982

FINE PRINT, Cafeteria-Style

The 'birds of the air' will fly in from north, south east, west. A veritable small press movement will be underway.

Dear Alec
I am thrilled that you liked my little comic. In fact, it was your story in Fast Fiction #2 which inspired me to print it myself...

You will have no trouble separating the innovators from the novelty-hunters.

I don't want Alec in our comic after this issue. He's too conservative, all his pictures in neat little boxes.

That will be a recurrent theme; Guys with one eye on the coolometer And myopic guys, dilletantes, pretenders, complete wankers, sweethearts, boy geniuses. They'll all traffic past you.

Ilya, the entrepreneur in this realm of D.I.Y. publishing: every nihilist young pencil's connected and he's the wiring.

Biff, role model, antecedent: he's manufacturing his cartoons onto t-shirts, drinking mugs and postcards and hawking them from a street-market stall at Camden Lock.

A mysterious, nameless religious nut's pamphlet tells us vitamins are an alien invasion from outer space.

Get schoolmasterish Lock to review your comic in his fanzine. He writes it all under pseudonyms like Christine Padgett, and his masterpiece, Reg Uspatoff.

Myra will turn up with her venomous little punky vicious characters. She's the opposite.

The guy who can't draw but is in great demand because he can drive and pick up boxes from the printer. (Real artists are useless in that department): He'll do a comic called CRIME with a micro-comic freebie insert called PETTY CRIME. Everybody's got at least one good idea.

People you never meet but whose work you keep an eye on over the years, like Helen Cusack, who's always being lumped in with the feminist crowd: You'll come across one of her books in a remainder-shop years later in Australia.

INCENSED NUDES (AFTER PICASSO)
Helen Cusack

"What's she doing now?" you'll ask.

Mail Art will be in for a while. An entity designating himself BU TO SA HO sends out postcard-sized cuttings from huge billboards.

Somebody will use a highlighter pen to attract eyes to a cover blurb and suddenly hand-coloured covers are the thing. Ilya will help you do a run of 350 copies, several colours plus strokes of tippex correction white. You're an artist. Things are flying this way and that. Every month you've got at least one story in print. You won't even remember half of it.

It is essential that in the middle of all this you meet your future wife.

FATE will land her from Australia in the middle of the London tube strike.

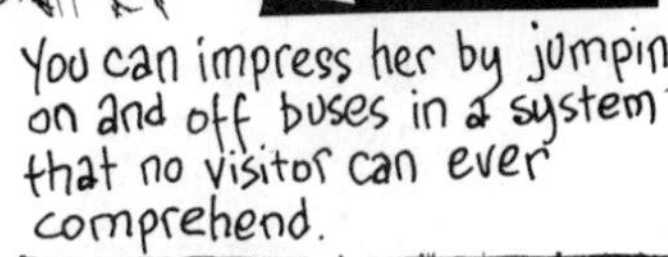

You can impress her by jumping on and off buses in a system that no visitor can ever comprehend.

Wind up at the WORLD'S END in Chelsea and play the juke box. Whatever's on there will have to be "our song" forever. So choose quickly, but wisely.

Life is sure to get very ramshackle from here on. Annie will be sleeping on a friend's floor in Earl's Court. (your brother's girl friend's)

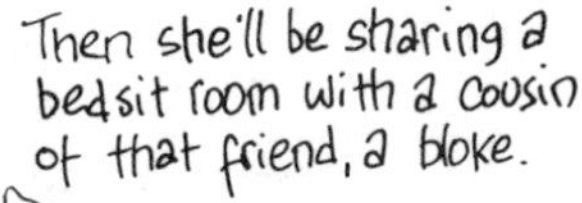

Then she'll be sharing a bedsit room with a cousin of that friend, a bloke.

Three of his pals will arrive from Australia and they'll all sleep on the floor of the single room. Merry Christmas.

your funds will be getting low by now and ART isn't buttering any crumpets. You'll have advanced from self-publishing to letting others do it for you.

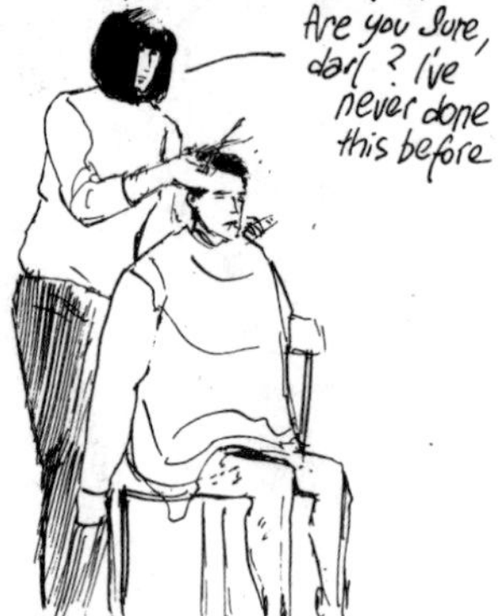

Are you sure, darl? I've never done this before

You may notice that your appearance is getting a bit dull. You're wearing a faded old jacket your mother bought for you when you were fourteen.

Your old pal Harwood will inform you that the old bloke in the flat next door to him has left for good for America. Help yourself to a scarf and a clothes brush. Thank you, old bloke

Even the shine has gone off the Man at the Crossroads. By necessity he starts taking a wee percentage from the table, bless him.

One night you'll propose setting up house with Annie.

There will be the side-benefit of cutting the expense of running back and forth to London.

You will at this stage find it necessary to defraud the government. You might pretend for instance that you're lodging with your old pal Danny Grey so you can continue to pick up the dole money.

Danny's your 'mentor' from those five years working in the factory cutting sheet metal into rectangles for ducting.

You see, FATE sees to it that you get an early intimation of your role.

The world will beat a path to your door
ah stop.
It's just a fact.

you'll be sleeping with Annie in their spare room.

Alec! wake up!
Danny's got into bed behind me.
oh shit! For God's sake don't wake him up. Just go back to sleep.
What's he wearing?
Don't bloody wake him up.

And in the morning

Danny's gone out. He said he was too embarassed to face you. What on earth's he done this time?

The ideas will fly about like insects to a flame.

Hey look what Elliott's done. He's bounced that one right back at me.

Annie will bust the photocopier at her place of employment while running off one of your last self-published items.

You're playing house-husband till the breakthrough comes

The man at the Crossroads will introduce you to his lover. You didn't even know he was gay.

They're living together in Fulham. This guy has a nice production job at the magazine Harper and Queen, which pays the rent. A plan is about to hatch over the camomile tea. and the conspicuously well-made shoes.

It will be an ambitious plan, to be sure.

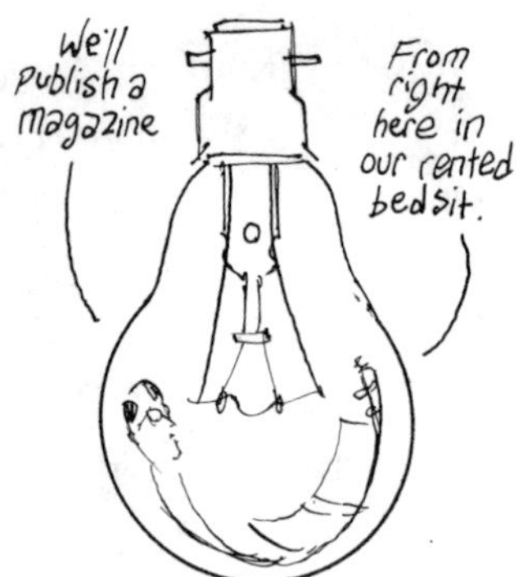

We'll publish a magazine
From right here in our rented bedsit.

They will corral all the talent and promise of the Fast Fiction table and put it in a magazine which they will launch in the new year.

A showcase for yourself, Elliott... those who are doing work of real value

They're rounding it up from hither and yon. You didn't know so much was happening...

And others I haven't had time to introduce to you yet. I'm meeting new people every week. I'm certain that we're on the verge of something important.

Designy typography stuff like Rian Hughes is doing...

© R. Hughes.

...or Shaky Kane's hip funny stuff...

WILD BILL BURROUGHS
by Shaky Kane
SINCE THE FINAL ACADEMY, I'M GETTING THE RECOGNITION I DESERVE!
I THOUGHT JACK BENNY WAS DEAD...

© Shaky Kane

...or Savage Pencil's graphic spittle

MY FAVORIT TOO. A TONIC FOR ONES BOWELLS! ALWAYS...
LOOK MATE I THINK YOU OUGHT TO KNOW THAT I THINK YOU'RE A BIG JAKOFF A POSIN' PILLUK. AN' I'M A FRAUD I AINT VORTY AT ALL I'M JUST A REGULAR INSECURE, KINDA GUY WITH NOTHIN' BETTA TO DO THAN FOLLA FASHION!!

© Pencil

It's the early '80s It's Thatcher's Britain

YAHOO

You run through Epping Forest in the nude (after Annie)

You're an artist, after all

So what in blazes is it anyway ?

Chapter Two

I don't mean : is this Art ?

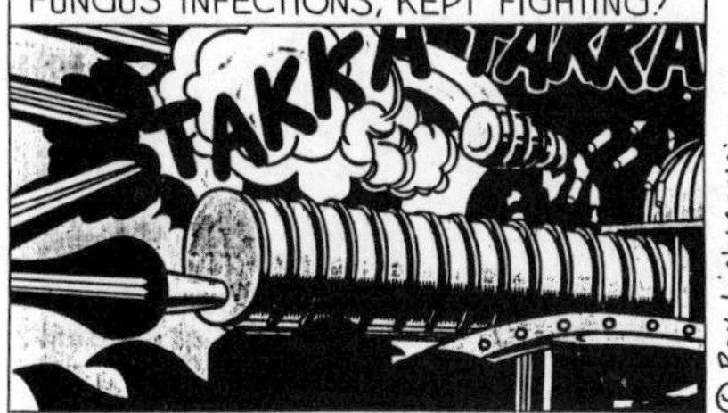

THE EXHAUSTED SOLDIERS, SLEEPLESS FOR FIVE AND SIX DAYS AT A TIME, ALWAYS HUNGRY FOR DECENT CHOW, SUFFERING FROM THE TROPICAL FUNGUS INFECTIONS, KEPT FIGHTING!
TAKKA TAKKA

© Roy Lichtenstein.

And is this not ?

ON GUADALCANAL, THE EXHAUSTED MARINES, SLEEPLESS FOR FIVE AND SIX DAYS AT A TIME, ALWAYS HUNGRY FOR DECENT CHOW, SUFFERING FROM THE TROPICAL FUNGUS INFECTIONS, KEPT ON FIGHTING!
TAKKA TAKKA

© prob. D.C. Comics.

It's all bloody aRt as far as you're concerned, Alec MacGarry

And the question is a semantic splitting of hairs, as mighty Alan Moore will say, more or less

Whether he will speak it or write it is not likely to be later recalled.

But what is it made of ? How does it happen ? A person, the artist, sees or hears a thing in his or her brain and strives to make it exist outside of there. simple.

But how did it get in there and arrange itself just so, the stuff in his or her noggin, presuming it wasn't lifted wholesale from somebody else like with that writer who had to give her prize back.

you will have cultivated your own chosen little plants on the great plains of the past and present, little shoots among the grass and the big world hardly even knows the grass is there

The shoots connect by fragile root systems one to another and then to yourself, informing a particular vision of the world.

Astonishing. Why does nobody else see it just so.?

One day you will spy somebody else watering the same wee shoots.

HEY, YOU!

And all your youthful idealism will burst out in a great big lovely messy salad.

Status Quo will raise objection to the sloppy lack of discipline among ye young upstarts, as tho the small press were a matter for consumer debate, like bus timetables. (How perceptive, to see a threat so far off)

I don't agree with the proposition that if a story is true there is no need to make it convincing

He'll probably be only at the beginning of his own career, otherwise he wouldn't even be aware of your existence, but at this stage of your life, anyone who's made a living at it for a year and a half is an old pro.

But somebody's got to play Darth Vader.

It will strike you as odd, his unflinching willingness to adopt the reactionary point of view, artistic suicide in this Age of the neurosis of innovation.

This guy's a larf

Doesn't he know that posterity pillories such types indiscriminately. Better to read your grocery list on stage,

He obviously doesn't know you like I do.

or go down Main Street chained back to back with three other people. The Frat initiation has hijacked art.

For the love of Beta Zeta Pi

They have no sense of the history.

Comics, if not this hobbyist thing, like collecting bottle-caps, is mostly this very conservative, nostalgia-for-childhood thing

Some Guys learn to draw just so they can fulfil the ambition of being hired to continue the adventures of their childhood Hero which is all very nice and they are among the most unassuming, agreeable people.

But *Status Quo* will have missed the fact that you have inserted yourself in a broader, bigger picture.

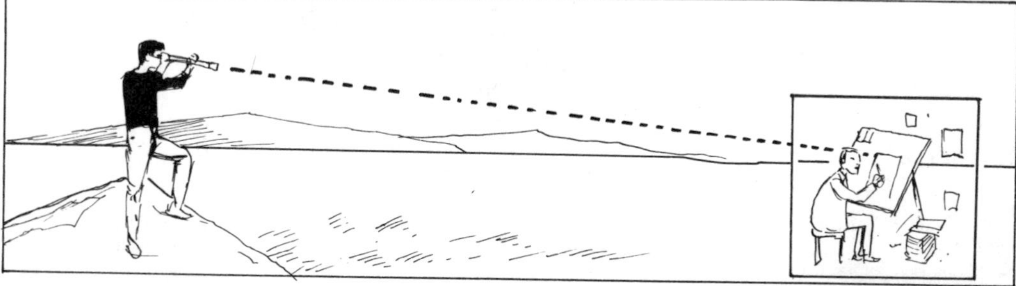

But you'll need some money so you can continue the self-delusion that you are making your way as an artist rather than a pretzel.

My God you'll be a couple of years short of 30 and still think of everybody else, even your contemporaries as a generation ahead. Why'd it take so long?

There could be *Knockabout*, the Underground guys, peddling boffo yocks around the open air concerts. It's only got to be funny.

Here's the Careers officer, whose job it is to head off any foolish notions.

But the people who draw comics are people who aimed higher and failed. They wanted to be in advertising or animation. Why don't you...

So you'll pore over their books trying to find something funny. Wee Hunt Emerson's funny most of the time, but it's another time, somebody else's.

Oook-yeah!... THAT FEELS LOTS BETTER!
© Emerson

(The career comic-book artist had not yet trod the stage, but was just about to, and after him, the comic-book bohemian)

COMICS AS A MEDIUM FOR SELF EXPRESSION? OH JOHN, YOU'RE SUCH A FOOL!
I-I'M SORRY!
RAW

© Spiegelman

Arch bohemian Spiegelman will have just started serializing his *Maus* in the U.S.A., after spending most of the seventies editing novelties for a bubble-gum co. The man at the Crossroads will compel you to read it.

As Curt Vile he will have added to that a half-page spot in the weekly national rock paper SOUNDS, sharing the page with Savage Pencil

Everybody will be wanting Moore. He'll be simultaneously writing for all 3 of the publishers of American-style Heroic comics He'll get big fat Marvel U.K., in the interests of fanning local flames, to run small-press reviews.

INE REVIEWS
by alan moore

fanzine space is given over entirely to the not inconsiderable outpourings ...T GEN, a multi-media empire making an attempt at global domination!

·EA BEHIND PRO-IS . . . is to arrive at ...ated entirely by its ...ce. So, if you're an ...mic strip writer who ...artist, or an artist in ...writer, or a poet, or ...ur musician, or a pre-...e tatooist or indeed ...else that's interesting ...legal, get in touch with ...ple at GEN by dropping a

...HILLYER, 13 FRESHFIELD ..., TRENT GARDENS, ...THGATE, LONDON N14

GEN 2
34 loose-leaf pages, £1.00 inc. postage from Ed Hillyer, address left

I saw the first issue of Gen a few months ago and must admit to not being terribly impressed. It

With this second issue, most of my initial doubts have gone the way of all flesh. This is a remarkably entertaining package containing strips, poetry, illustration, music reviews, handy home hints, eight free postcards and a liberal smattering of fear, loathing and boffo yoks.

That's not to say that there weren't bits I enjoyed more than

There's a sort of foaming-at the-mouth brain-damaged energy at play here, and I find that entirely commendable. I shall be watching out for this one in the months to come. Then, I can rip off all the good, original ideas that come up and get paid vast sums of money for them while the creators languish in squalor and obscurity. I'm sorry. That's just the sort of person I am . . .

ACES No.1
A four page broadsheet-cum-scrapbook of deranged oddities, available for 10p and a first class stamp from Ed Hillyer, address above.

© Moore.

Alan Moore will be the great anomaly. He'll be caught up with the Hero boys at this stage.

For a laugh Vile and Pencil will have swapped places for one week. Pencil will have continued Vile's characters admirably but Vile will have killed off all the charges entrusted to him

Here he will write a piece on one of the books you will have done with Ilya and through Ilya you'll receive a very important communication.

But he is to be an artist of high merit. He will have started by selling the weekly Maxwell the Magic Cat to his local paper, the *Northants Post*, under the name Jill de Ray, a 'frustrated bitch' according to one reader.

Savage will thereafter have put down his pencil and drawn no more comic strips in Sounds

more or less

or so legend will have it.

The guy who will hand you your travelling ticket for the next leg; you will not even be aware he's been watching you.

You'll have been watching him too, an unmistakable figure in the Westminster Arms, unofficial creative H.Q. of the bi-monthly comic marts, especially after his photo was in the first issue of Skinn's ambitious WARRIOR magazine. Oddly, a lager drinker.

You'll exchange a great many thoughts with this creative juggernaut, insofar as anyone is able, in that melee, and this before anybody was a 'star'.

You'll visit with him at his home in Northants a month later, mooching a lift from truck driver Danny Grey on one of his far-flung deliveries.

Good Grief, It's Danny Grey

JUST FOR AN INSTANT I HAVE THE SENSE OF PANEL BORDERS LOOMING ON THE PERIPHERY OF MY VISION

..FRAMING ME, the LORRY, THE HANDSHAKE, THE SAINSBURY'S CARRIER BAG IN MY OTHER HAND, The INFANTS SCHOOL OVER THE ROAD...

The Moore household will be a chaotic thing.

At the end of every night Alan and Phyllis will round up all the tiles of the fireplace and put them back where they belong.

Never cement them or glue them down or anything, just arrange them loosely back in their places.

Doesn't that broken bit go with that other broken bit?

Another person will turn up to share the living room floor...

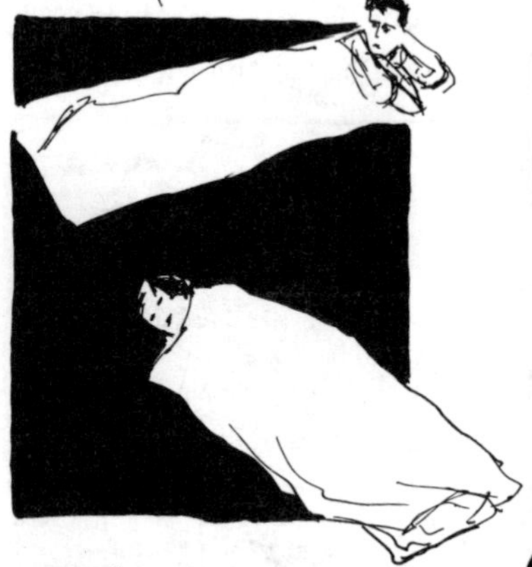

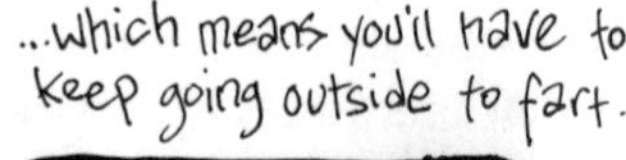

...which means you'll have to keep going outside to fart.

You will feel on the doorstep of an important revelation.

And will consequently append your contract with Fate:

Security will be high in London in these days. Metal doors will open, but not until you've sweated a bit.

Down through busy magazine production offices, feeling very self-conscious.

into the inner Sanctum

No this isn't what I expected.

Getting out will seem an even longer hike.

It's a bit squirmy to go and miss a wide open goal in full view of people whose opinion matters.

Bryan Talbot will get the Sounds spot. He'll call it *Scumworld* and go under the alias *Bryan Talbot and the crabs from Uranus*. You will observe that the requirement here is a raffish quality which is not your metier. To hell with art, you will resolve, and bugger the metier while you're at it.

You'll finish off one set of samples into a readable story and send them to a small press publisher named Sharp up in Manchester, one of Ilya's multifarious connections.

There's a second set of samples you composed after the initial rejection but these will fail to elicit any kind of response. Yesterday you were being turned down, now you're beneath notice.

These ones will not even be funny. You'll send them to *Knockabout* where they'll be immediately accepted to appear December.

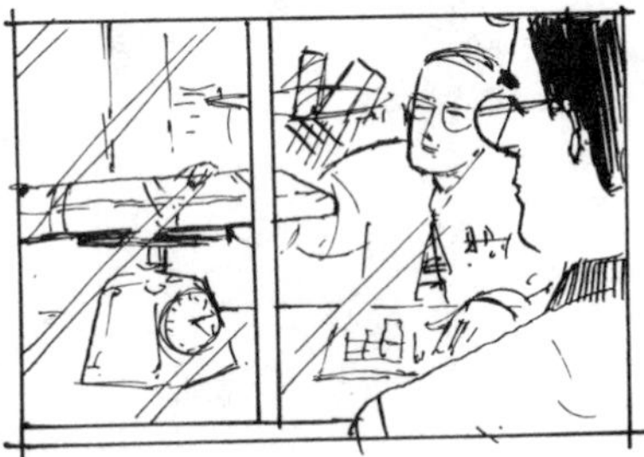

You are one of those animals of which nothing goes to waste. Your hooves go to the glue factory and your head makes margarine.

The Man at the Crossroads will have got the first issue of *Escape* magazine printed. It will be well received all over the place.

It will be reviewed in an Arts magazine on a big tabloid page split equally among reviews of: a new translation of Cellini, a study of the architect who designed the Oxo stock cube building like an Oxo stock cube, and Escape magazine, with a reproduction of one of your pieces.

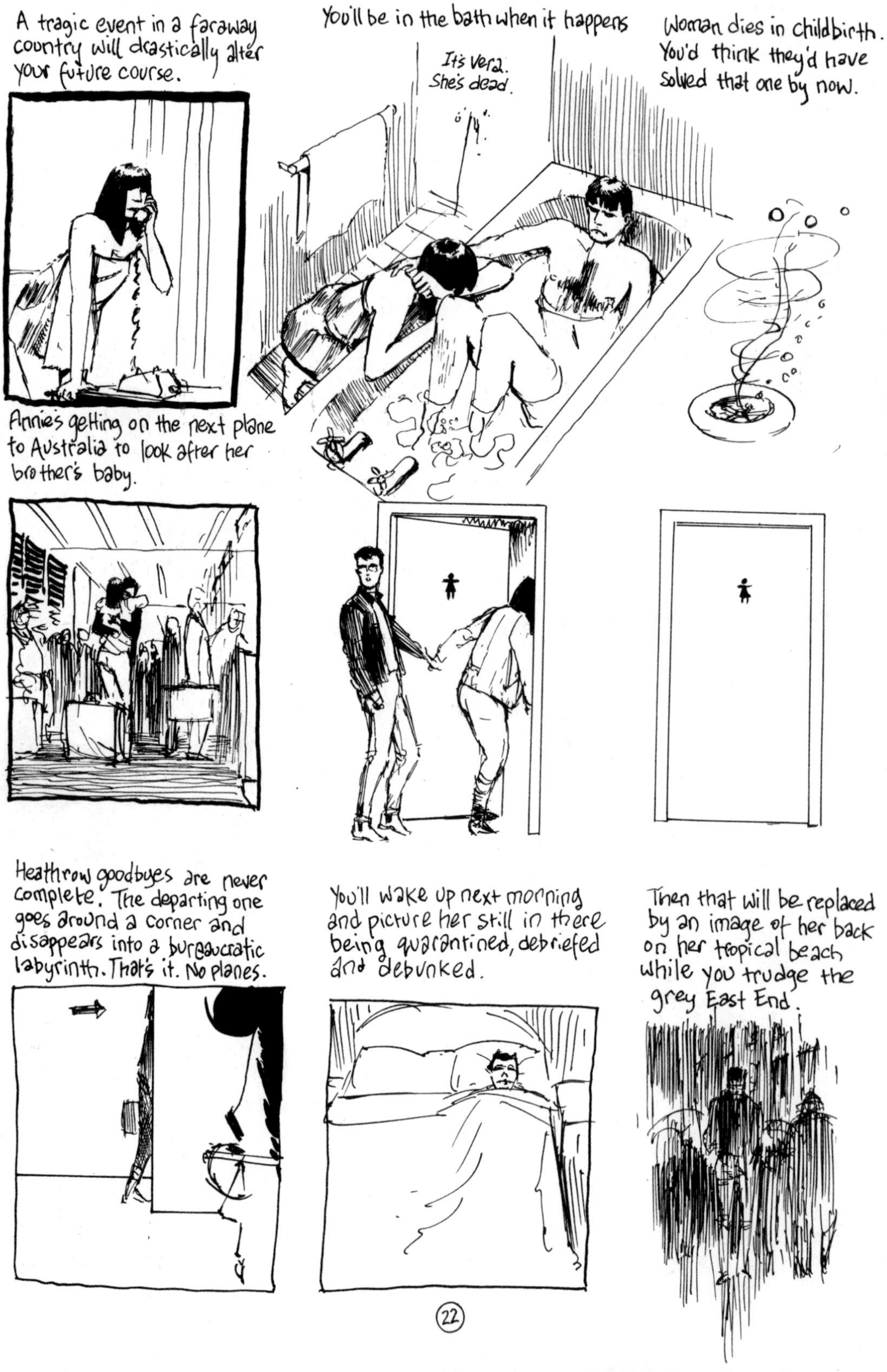

A tragic event in a faraway country will drastically alter your future course.

Annie's getting on the next plane to Australia to look after her brother's baby.

You'll be in the bath when it happens

It's Vera. She's dead.

Woman dies in childbirth. You'd think they'd have solved that one by now.

Heathrow goodbyes are never complete. The departing one goes around a corner and disappears into a bureaucratic labyrinth. That's it. No planes.

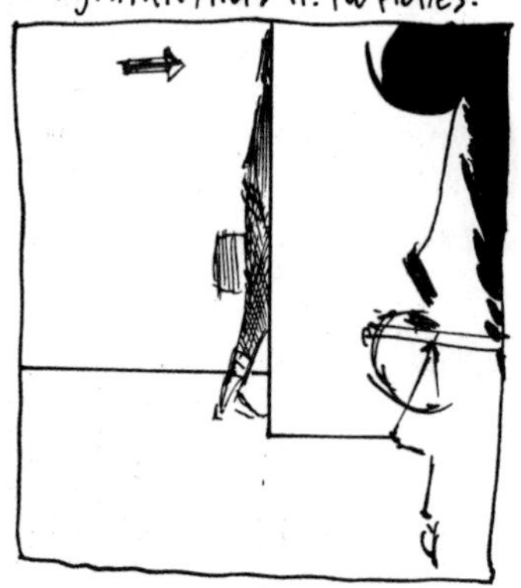

You'll wake up next morning and picture her still in there being quarantined, debriefed and debunked.

Then that will be replaced by an image of her back on her tropical beach while you trudge the grey East End.

CHEMIST

Chapter Three

The resolve to be, to the exclusion of all else, an artist, will be a difficult one to maintain.

You will have immediately gone into free-fall, with the ground rushing up at an alarming speed.

You may find that you start to lose patience with the bargain you made with FATE.

ya bastard! ya forgot me! Just give me one sign, let me hold the cash from one sale of my work! Just one!

This will be your second lapse of faith, Alec MacGarry.

Then Annie's unscheduled return to Australia will have precipitated an hour of crisis.

You can't pay the rent on your own so you'll call the landlord and try to wrap it up without pain.

I rented this to Anne as a favour. You're not even supposed to be here.
Come on, man, this is difficult enough.

You'll go up north to Blackpool and live with your parents again after all this time.

You'll get a job in a seafront nightclub and save some money.

Did anybody hand in a set of false teeth last night? this is so embarrassing.

The *Escape* Summer issue will arrive late in the mail: 3-D section, spectacles and everything. Yourself, Elliott, Kane, Emerson, Hughes, Myra. The gang's all here. But your mind will be elsewhere.

The night sky will be calling you across the sea.

i'll go round the world and bring her back.

But to leave when i'm so close to cracking it.

is life intimidating Art or is Art intimidating Life?

I've never borrowed money from my father before.

Dad, I want to go to Australia but I haven't got enough money.

Do they still do the "Assisted passage"

Eh? the "£10 assisted passage" that finished in the 'sixties. I envision my Dad saying:

Here's twenty. Take Danny with you.

You'll meet up with Ilya in a hilltop cottage in Derbyshire.

we've covered so much ground over the last year... Now i'm off to college and you're going abroad.
...sniff... To a hot place.

Have you got any of the hand-coloured Xmas cards left? We could get 'em out again this year.

Those bloody cards. They'd have been alright if you hadn't put them in cling-wrap.

fghlubb

How was I to know the Pictures would peel off? selling photocopied Art is a new game altogether.

You'll be on your way to Australia, Alec MacGarry...

...But it will be a good idea to stop over in London for the first official meeting of *Escape* magazine, publishers and contributors.

They will have hired an upstairs room at a pub.

You and I would just go in the bar, Alec MacGarry, but factionalism will have already taken its hold.

They don't want every Tom, Dick and Harry getting mixed up in it.

A guy named Dakin's here.

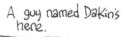

He will be surprised that everyone will know his stuff. But that's how it is when your stuff's the right stuff. He'll pull his first photocopied comic out of a plastic bag.

Portfolio Cases? Nobody here uses one. That must be another faction you're thinking of.

Dakin will have appeared in a crap glossy expensive comic called *pssst!* which will have had the man at the Crossroads for a sub-editorial gopher at the time when he first sent out his various communications

pssst! will have systematically rejected everything of value that came its way (except Dakin, curiously) including yourself. Almost too uncanny to be coincidental. Fate will have placed it there to test everybody's patience.

There will always be a *pssst!*, though it may go by another name in your own epoch, preaching the 'Art' of comics while squandering the potential of the market on its foolish inanities before collapsing under the weight of expensive folly.

It will also have *psssd off* the hoary old pros at the *Society of Strip Illustrators* by inviting them to compete for the prize of designing the *pssst* logo, instead of hiring someone to do it, treating them like a mob of young hopefuls.

Naturally one of the hoary old pros will have rubbished the magazine in their own monthly SSI Journal.

The man at the Crossroads will have obtained for you a copy to peruse. There's a member in the correspondence columns beefing about coming all the way down from the Orkneys with his good lady wife for the annual dinner and some of the members haven't even bothered to hire tuxedos.

...offence to the dignity of his good lady and all that.

The SSI is an association of professionals. Acceptance to membership will require that the applicant have made a living from comics for one year. *Status Quo* is the new chairman. They meet upstairs at a pub.

From the other side of the planet you can't see it.

Even at night, Darwin airport will be a steam bath. It may cause you to consider how climate would influence national temperament, or it may not.

At Townsville Annie will meet you and ensconce you in the Travelodge for the afternoon.

(It will have been six months after all)

Then in Ingham you will meet her charge, the motherless child.

And there will be many beers at the house on the beach under the tropical sun with your future father-in-law and his remarkable fund of anecdotes

And there will be islands with nobody on them.

Can you be an artist not connected with any 'Art World'? Can you be one if nobody ever knows it?

Here's one of those anecdotes:

Among several poems by one Dan Sheahan, sugar cane farmer, published in the *North Queensland Register* was, in 1944, one titled *The Pub Without Beer*.

It is lonely away from
your kindred and all,
In the bushland at
night when the
warrigals call
Regis

In 1957, one Gordon Parsons, timber man and country singer, comes upon the basis of the poem aurally, and, believing it to be public domain 'folk' material, sets about constructing it into a workable song.

Get this down:
Oh, it's lonesome away from your kindred and all, By the campfire at night, where the wild dingoes call ...

That year it is recorded by his mate Slim Dusty when he's a song short of his quota at a session. It becomes a million seller, his first hit, and a big surprise to himself. It does well in Britain too but probably remains unheard in America.

But there's nothing so lonesome, morbid or drear...

The story goes that Sheahan's boys took the matter up with Dusty when he toured through Ingham. For half an hour the story is a cause celebre in musical circles and for slightly longer than that in the town of Ingham.

Than to stand in the bar of a pub with no beer.

Plagiarism? Artists adapt stuff all the time. It's just a bit embarrassing if it becomes a runaway hit. (It didn't seem to matter to anyone that the tune Parsons set the poem to was essentially *Beautiful Dreamer* with a country gait.)

Register
There's a faraway look on the face of the bum, While the barmaid glares down at the paint on her thumb.

But that's just copping a feel in comparison to the triumphal loss of virginity that will accompany the sale of your first story.

So send out your messages in bottles, one and all. Who knows what may come of it? *Caveat emptor.*

Right at this time, however, you will be working on the problem of raising a mere hundred. You'll have enough to get you through the three months but it'd be nice to have a bit more.

or strip, as Elliott calls them.

Alec, can you do us another strip?

Years previously you will have painted some designs on some leather jackets for five quid a pop.

By now your "virginity" will weigh heavily upon your soul, and here is how you will set about losing it: ...

The British Comics "Small Press thing" will be starting to make international connections. There are some guys in Canada doing their own thing and a girl in Tokyo. Elliott will have sold some sticker designs to Fiorucci in Italy.

An Australian guy, Beardy Bentley of Melbourne, will have been in London, heard the word and taken it back with him.

He will have been corresponding with you for a year now. You'll call him up North.

You're a guest here, so he'll be a guest of a guest. You will watch, with amazement at his adeptness, his dismantlement of a quiche into its encyclopedic components.

He'll be one of a team putting out a comics mag called INKSPOTS which, if truth be told, will be nearer the pssst model than any other.

You'll put it to him that in his, uh, editorial capacity, he might like to patronise a worthy artist to the tune of one hundred frogskins.

...and take away with him the originals of a four-pager you'll have been busy drawing about 'The Pyjama Girl', an infamous Australian murder.

And there you'll do the deal. You'll make your first ever sale. On a tropical beach.

Full of yourself, you will then drink too many beers and put your head through the fluorescent tube in the garage.

With the taste of impending celebrity in your saliva you'll be eager to get back to London.

It'll be the pull of gravity.

Annie will cry though she leaves the baby in competent hands.

You'll propose marriage at Darwin airport.

In London you'll drop in on the Escape boys and have showers. Dakin will be visiting.

You'll confess to him that you feel you shouldn't have been away from the hub of things for so long

If you weren't here you were somewhere else.

That remarkable thought will splash through your brain.

If I wasn't here I was somewhere else.

what a deliciously egocentric notion.

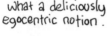

The most interesting place is where you are.

In the days when you had to make your own entertainment.

it's funny how the people on the top deck of the bus go past our second storey window like that
I'm going to show them your bum.
Not if I show them yours first.

You're killing time waiting for your book to come out.

THE LIFE AND TIMES OF
ALEC
McGARRY 2
WITH AN INTRODUCTION BY ALAN MOORE

(c) campbell. Escape.

The Escape boys are being fussy and finicky in their publishing of it.

We can reverse this out and burn off that and bla...
Let's have another cup of nettle tea.

It'll be an Ice-Age of waiting.
Take your mind off it.

You'll be down on the South Coast at Easter with Danny Grey and co.

Annie will say:

. To think that France is just across that water. A whole other country. In Australia we're so isolated

SHUT UP.

Wouldn't it be so easy...

Shut up for god's sake they'll do it.

So next thing you've got day-return passports, virtually all your cash is gone and you're looking into the steely grey of the English channel

Prendergast's hanging off the rail for a photo.

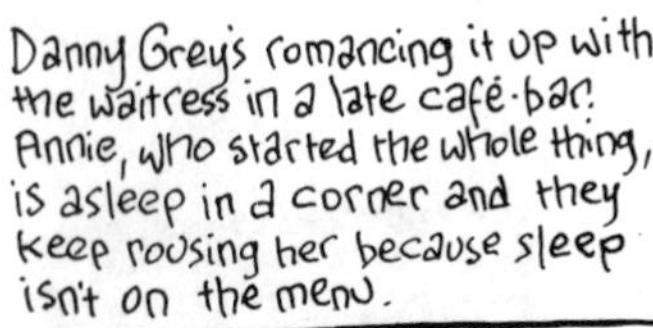
Danny Grey's romancing it up with the waitress in a late café-bar. Annie, who started the whole thing, is asleep in a corner and they keep rousing her because sleep isn't on the menu.

im the English Pilot and you're Mamzel Marie of the rayzeestawnce

You'll miss the last ferry and have to crash in the transit depot.

You'll wake up only thinking of the book: "Danny Grey never really forgave himself for leaving Alec MacGarry asleep at the turnpike."

It'll be an Ice Age waiting for a candle to flicker.

For a shining moment you'll be a novelty and you can only be that once.

Your first feeling upon seeing your first proper book will be disappointment. Getting beyond the hand-made photocopied things turns out to be no big deal.

From that moment the concept of "book" will hold no value and you will often buy expensively bound books and think nothing of cutting them up. If an idiot like you can be published, there can't be any inherent authority in the form.

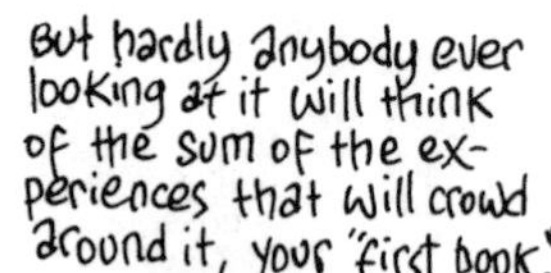

But hardly anybody ever looking at it will think of the sum of the experiences that will crowd around it, your "first book."

You'll be on a London Radio Arts program, stuck in behind playwright Alan Ayckbourn. They'll ask him about his themes; they'll ask you what made you want to draw a comic.

Worse than that, they'll play you in with Queen's theme to *Flash Gordon*, the most audible contemporary example of comicstripiana.

bzz War-rocket Ajax approaching
Fizz buzz z
bzzz
AW SHIT

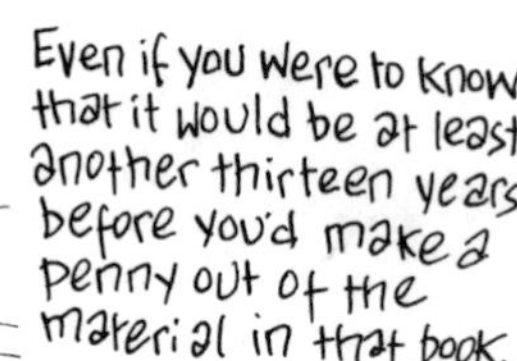

Even if you were to know that it would be at least another thirteen years before you'd make a penny out of the material in that book...

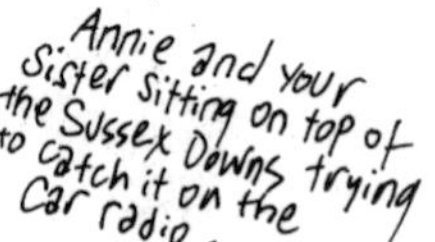

Annie and your sister sitting on top of the Sussex Downs trying to catch it on the car radio.

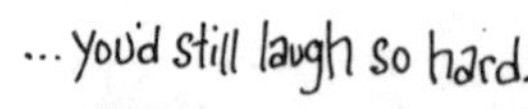

... you'd still laugh so hard.

A Mayfair gallery wakes up one morning with the idea that comic books are the next page in the story of ART.

An assemblage of the new comics and some paintings influenced by comics. They'll get hold of the Man at the Crossroads for the 'New Comics'.

I couldn't help overhearing...
GIMPEL FILS GALLE

Don't ask how he always pops up when he's needed, or descends from a passing cloud

I rather fancy reading a comic, Jeremy.
I was in the neighbourhood...

So it'll be the real McCoy, all the right people. From the Comics camp at any rate.

Spiegelman will be on that wall...

I WAS EXPECTED TO COMFORT HIM!
MOTHER... MOTHER...
© Spiegelman.

And Biff,

LATER, I TRAVELLED WIDELY.
NOT ANOTHER CULTURAL IMPERIALIST!
IN AFRICA, THEY USED TO CALL ME "THE WHITE NEGRO". I'LL TAKE THE FRIED EGG SANDWICH PLEASE.
© Biff

And Oscar Zarate, Savage Pencil, Myra, Anarchist Cliff Harper...

3 WHAT IS GOVERNMENT?
© Harper.

I DECLARE THEM TO BE MY ENEMY . . .

© Harper

And Alec MacGarry will be asleep again at the turnpike.

"When the neurotics appropriated the strip cartoon," says the Arts Correspondent in *The Guardian*, Waldemar Januszcak, "we witnessed an ideal marriage of form and content. They subverted its innocence and filled its thought balloons with their wretched, guilt-sodden soliloquies."

In another time and place and with a different bunch of people there would now be a group proclaiming themselves *The Neurotics* but this lot are too busy agonizing about whether it's hip to be in a posh Mayfair gallery.

THE NEWROTIC

The *New Musical Express* man Watson's at the opening party too. He tapes a chat with you. For a couple of years Comics will be a hip sub-culture.

Big Argentinian Oscar Zarate tags along on that one.

It's all International. Waiting to happen in a lot of places all at once.

Oscar's the illustrator on one of Anne Tauté's Comic book Shakespeare Volumes: the *Othello*.

–O, CURSE OF MARRIAGE, THAT WE CAN CALL THESE DELICATE CREATURES OURS AND NOT THEIR APPETITES! I HAD RATHER BE A TOAD, AND LIVE UPON THE VAPOUR OF A DUNGEON, THAN KEEP A CORNER IN THE THING I LOVE FOR OTHERS' USES.
© Zarate.

The valiant lady re-mortgaged her house to raise 90,000 quid to set herself up as a publisher and do this series.

At the opening party she has a bandage on her face. The only time you ever meet her she has a bust nose.

You and Annie will be lodging with your sister in Brighton. You'll have got yourself a short-term job filing soldiers' medical records.

Then the floodgates open. You land a weekly spot in Sounds.

You won't even have to go up there this time. Savage Pencil in his everyday on-staff guise of Edwin Pouncey will send word via the *Man at the Crossroads* that the spot's open again.

Every time there's a new editor the first thing he does is toss out the cartoons. They like to mark their territory and this will offend the least people. That's a double-edged sword but never mind.

So you'll get Elliott on the phone and lay out a plan. He'll have had a spot in the *Melody Maker* for four weeks while you were in Australia. He knows these things aren't easy to hold onto.

FABBO-DINKUMS!

BUSBY'S
ROCK & POP FACTS
THE RECENT DISCO DANCE CRAZE OF 'BODY-POPPING WAS IN FACT INITIATED BY L.P. LIME OF THE JACKSON VILLE ASYLUM. "HE SPENDS HOURS DANCING AND TWITCHING IN HIS ROOM" SAYS L.P.'S NURSE.
© Elliott

© Elliott

So rather than be in competition for the gig, you'll create a phony cartoonist, Charlie Trumper and take turns in ghosting for him.

I'll do all the lettering and sign them, so nobody'll be any the wiser.

The Wonders of Science. It's in a Music Paper and its got nothing to do with music. What a joy.

Which came first? The bacon or the egg
How should I know
© Charlie 84 Trumper

It's got nothing to do with Science either, for that matter.

THE WONDERS OF SCI
I'M PROFESSOR BEAN and I love the Government
I'M a six-fingered clone of Harry McGinnis and I love the Government
I'm Rubbery Rodney and I love the Government
I'm a logo
I'm a dog and I love the Government
I'm a pain in the arse
I'm an egg-cup

With your interview in the NME you'll get invited to fill up the 'THRILLS', or guest cartoonist spot for a month with your autobiographical nonsense. They've been running some hot new American Cartoonists in there like Seattle's Lynda Barry.

IS THERE SOMETHING YOU'RE TRYING TO TELL ME MYRNA?
ED BREAD
© Barry.

And Mark Beyer, of RAW

LATER AT A HOSPITAL
THE PILLS MUST HAVE BEEN CONTAMINATED!
© Beyer.

Punk pamphleteer Holmstrom, J.D. King, Bagge,... what a rich variety of voices is in the air.

HONEST! I WANNA DANCE WITH YOU!
I WOULDN'T DANCE WITH YOU IF YOU PUT A GUN TO MY HEAD!
© Holmstrom

Dakin will be visiting. You'll get him in on it and bang out a half dozen pieces.

And there, with a testament to your brilliance, will be his drawings.

"If MacGarry's quirky line-drawings seem primitive at first, they soon establish a charm of their own."

AT THE EURYTHMICS CONCERT I MET THIS INCREDIBLE GIRL.. SHE WAS UNBELIEVABLE IT WAS THE SWEETEST NIGHT OF MY LIFE!!
BENNET'S
© Dakin

They say these oh-so perceptive things but they can't tell the difference
charlie Trumper ©91

In one week, MacGARRY ghosts for Trumper, Dakin ghosts for MacGARRY and everybody goofs off on the beach.

Goofing off. You know, one of the things America has given the world along with the endless coffee refill, is a colourful bunch of expressions for doing nothing.

Like 'hanging out' and 'goofing off'.

Big Hairy Alan Moore's now writing for the Americans and taking them by storm.

Alright, here goes

They were probably all goofing off and hanging about when he landed among them like a hungry wolf...

...doing violence to their cosy concepts of the mud-monster and the earnest super-being.

© D.C.Comics INC.

The Man at the Crossroads gets you to hook up with him to tape a conversation for Escape.

THOMAS PYNCHON!
HENRY MILLER!
© Escape

It'll happen at the Princess Louise. As you arrive you see a peculiar thing. There's a guy assessing the pub in his *"Real Ale Guide"*.

Weighing up how many 'traditionally brewed' beers are on tap, how many stars awarded, etc. etc.

A strange way indeed to measure the quality of a pub. Surely you should put your ear to the door and listen for sounds of jollity.

Everywhere you turn a door opens. Your sister will need a display for the *Electronic Point of Sale Expo* for which she's part of the organising team.

Your drawing gets blown up to eleven feet high in the foyer of the Hammersmith Exhibition Centre. In one month you're regular in two national rock weeklies and hanging in two choice spots in the capital.

You're not getting rich or anything though. Life goes on much the same.

The Five Fifteen goes past in ten seconds

Your favourite types of young artist will be social creatures, too often swopping their work with their fellows instead of selling it and 'getting ahead' or working all day flogging it and glogging down the takings with a hot pie.

One day, Alec, you'll be seeing your confreres grinning back at you from glossy magazines.

Chapter Five

The media makes no differentiation between the national daily leftwing cartoonist Steve Bell...

...and anarchic vicious sometimes-cartoonist Savage Pencil, looking like Dracula's nephew.

...And Myra, selling her photocopied pamphlets at Camden Lock market in the manner of the Little Match Girl.

It's all shades of a colourful story to them.

Myra lands a spot in proximity to Bell in London's *City Limits* magazine doing her punk agony aunt *Miss March* on the letters page...

DEAR MISS MARCH,
I've been in LONDON for 7 mths now and I really can't see what people see in it. I haven't even seen anyone famous.

...dispensing anti-wisdom into the atmosphere.

Emerson's in this session too, in a graveyard or something

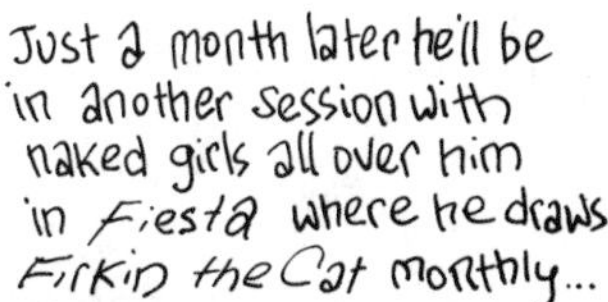

Just a month later he'll be in another session with naked girls all over him in *Fiesta* where he draws *Firkin the Cat* monthly...

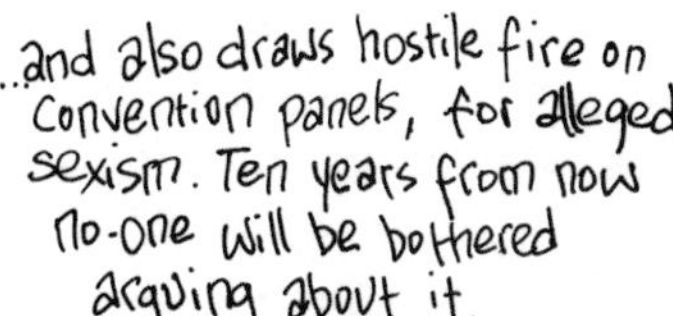

...and also draws hostile fire on Convention panels, for alleged sexism. Ten years from now no-one will be bothered arguing about it.

ANXIETY OVER SEX TAKES MANY FORMS – FOR EXAMPLE...

©Emerson

Emerson will give you Bell's number. They go back together to a small British underground Scene in the late seventies.

Bell will be living near you in Brighton. He's a disgruntled old anti-social creature who can't be talked into a meeting.

.. and you, the genius of the next generation: Alec MacGARRY: a man of destiny, no less.

One day the world will rush to borrow ten quid to have a drink with you.

Meanwhile you have a drink with Elliott, a talent to be reckoned with when he's not blowing himself over with cyclones of self-doubt.

...like at the London Con where they've given the small press crowd an hour and an audience.

ill put my bag in my room and meet you down stairs
okay
13

while you're throwing your bag in your hotel room, Elliott's done a runner back to Maidstone

Elliott gets an arty gig creating slide images for some performance artist in Dublin.

He has to go over there and do the work in situ.

By daybreak he's on a boat back again...

..envisioning himself putting his bags in Davy Jones' locker.

He'll make a comic of it, using his character Gimbley, shaking it up in a cocktail with metaphors and other discursive techniques.

Hughes doesn't borrow ten quid to drink with anyone, or at least he slips the tenner away for more important matters. Which is not to say he isn't a social creature.

He lands a harmless pussycat spot at the back of *Seventeen* magazine.

Produces his wee pamphlets at art-school's expense, like his mini-comic, ZIT. The man who names his work thus will years later design a typeface called:

FF Knobcheese™!

© Hughes.

His best work, for my money, is an unpublished page called *18 HOLES*, which has that number of little panels of almost abstract landscapes, each with a little triangular flag:

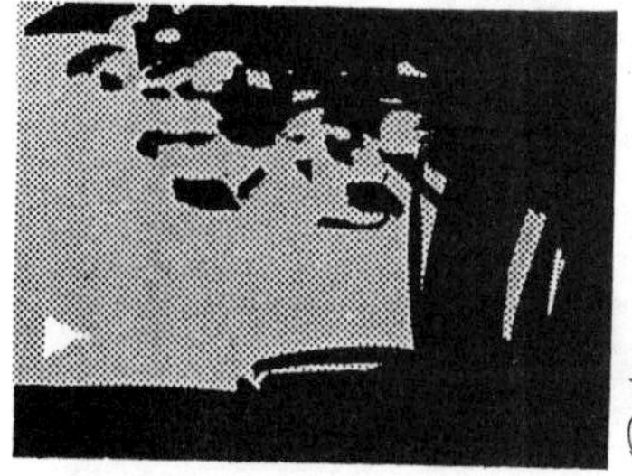

© Hughes.

Trevvy Trevs Phoenix puts out a one-shot comic called *Twenty Penguins*. He'll be the hippest, coolest dude you'll ever meet.

40p
TWENTY PENGUINS

© Phoenix

From the other side of the street he's wearing spats.

But close up it's a pair of low cut ladies' pumps over white socks.

It's that whole junk-shop chic of people who've been blithely getting along without money for too long.

Later you'll see Phoenix wearing second hand prescription eyeglasses, giving you one of those "That bullshit butters no parsnips with me, MacGarry" kind of looks, through another bloke's lenses.

You'll be having coffee with him another time and he coolly and with infinite hipness says:

ah, we should run away without paying.

and you being a bit older than these guys and afraid of looking too parental and neither hip nor cool...

Will take off at high speed

a delicious act of gratuitous delinquency.

You'll look back and, in spite of the distance, see him blush to the very roots of his being.

You'll have to go back and pick up the parsnips.

Dakin does a comic about flamenco buskers Forcione and Niebla.

The Musical Adventures of
EDUARDO NIEBLA
ANTONIO FORCIONE

© Dakin.

They sell it out of their guitar cases.

In I-D magazine there's a guy signing himself 'Wigan' draws big crowded cartoons where everybody's saying stuff.

© Wigan (detail)

I don't know that they ever say anything important or if it matters. "His poser-packed drawings immortalise the murky menagerie of late-night London hipsterdom" © NME

His cartoons are hung at the Garbanzo Coffee house for a month.

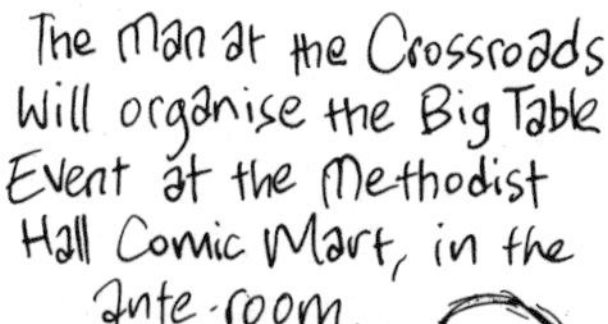

The Man at the Crossroads Will organise the Big Table Event at the Methodist Hall Comic Mart, in the ante-room.

Just about all of these artists and more will improvise live a variety of big pictures

...and work on each others' pictures...

...and do inspired things and daft things, though I challenge you to tell the difference.

SUDDENLY A TERRIFYING FACE CAME THROUGH THE WALL

At the SSI, *Status Quo* is in a sporty mood.

He arranges a confrontation between the professional fraternity and the young turks by inviting the latter to one of the monthly meetings at the George on the Strand, no doubt hoping to larn 'em something.

But the young guys just get along having a beer with the pros. Dakin's met a soccer comic writer whose work he admires

You'll have an admiring eye on big pro hairy Alan Moore, so impassioned in his view on the subject of Creators' Rights, that he's been called to shed light upon, that he doesn't notice his coat soaking up all the beer he spilled five minutes ago.

What a disappointing bunch of rebels you are.

But of course, the rebel thing's a journalistic myth. Young turks everywhere are probably living with their parents, ...

or holding down a Civil Service job. And it's only a 'story' if someone's kicking over the traces.

There's a lunch session in a beer garden next day. Savage Pencil enters.

He'll do a comic called *Nyak Nyak* along with Chris Long and Andy Johnson. Their press release will promise to 'overturn the torpid trestle' of the Alternative comics press.

MY GOODNESS! HE MEANS MY TABLE

Elsewhere he'll call your own book 'another nail in my coffin' while conceding that you're 'probably a nice bloke to have a cup of tea with'

YICK! YICK!

On the letters page of *Sounds* he'll make a personal appearance for the purpose of blowing away your *Professor Bean*.

SNORF BURLK
Well blow me if it isn't Savage Pencil. Don't see you in these pages very often any more-grin!
WELL I'M HERE AT TH' REQUEST OF READER ROSS MORGAN! SEEMS HE DON'T TAKE TO YOU AT ALL!
© Pencil
© Pencil

Now there's a worthy rebel. Of course he's also a staff journalist.

Speaking of *Sounds*, they've got a new editor. It's all change after 32 weeks.

Alec, the new editor doesn't "get" it. He wants us to do a "proper" comic.

So you'll switch to this, "the autobiography of the man who will destroy the world in 1985."

RODNEY:

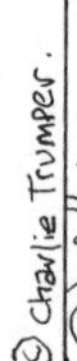

© Charlie Trumper.

It was quite early in my physical development that I noticed the curious device sharing my mother's womb with me....

And you'll do real rebellious stuff like having peoples arses exploding.

© Charlie Trumper.

You'll even start to influence your peers.

© Cooper.

You and Annie will sneak down to the Registry Office without telling anyone.

You'll stop a stranger to take the wedding photos. Annie's mother won't talk to her for a year and a half.

Well, it's either that or go to Australia and stand up and recite the usual nonsense.

You rebel, you.

Then you'll tour the country in your wee car, dining with your pals along the way.

Card from Dekin:

© Dakin.

Homage à Herriman
Krazy Kat © King Features.

Chapter Six

The cycle of renewal in Art is pedalled by the periodic influx of stuff from somewhere else. That's why you need a Man at the Crossroads

For three years he'll have been jabbering about what's going on in FRANCE. "La Ligne Claire" and all that.

One day they stop looking at all those *Druillet* monstrosities...

MINING ROBOTS! BUT CAN THEY STILL BE FUNCTIONING?
MMMMMM
OOOOOOO

© Druillet.

And decide that *Hergé's* the man to be with after all.

WOOU-HOUW-OU-OU-OU-WOOUUH!
!
!
?

Hergé 1948
©Editions Casterman

The man at the Crossroads conveys it to Elliott and Elliott spends the rest of his life drawing 'Clearlines'.

PERICLES THE PUNK WAS THROWING OUR PRECIOUS PORK PIES AT THE FLYING FISH ~

© Elliott '85

Serge Clerc will be one of the new French crop. In fact the NME will have been importing his little illustrations quite early

NME
WE POSE THE QUESTIONS AND QUESTION THE POSERS.

© clerc.

However, if you can read French, none of it is saying anything profound or memorable or even endearingly amusing on the level of Laurel and Hardy. It's just the next fashion.

The exception to the preceding, of course, is Claire Bretecher, who was translated in the *Sunday Times* magazine for a long while and has a page in *Cosmo* for a year.

The French government uses comics at the forefront of its cultural exchange abroad. Thus it will transpire that they've got an exhibition of French comics and a day long seminar at the *Institut Francais* in Queensberry Place and there's a private cocktail party at the apartments of the Cultural counsellor to the French Embassy. You're invited, Alec.

Druillet will be there in the flesh.

A History of the Comic Strip with Pierre Couperie, Maurice Horn and Claude Moliterni sorting out the chapters between them.

And Claude Moliterni. Now that will be interesting, bumping into him at this stage.

It was originally published as *Bande Dessinee et Figuration Narrative* and released to accompany an exhibition of comic art at the *Louvre* in 1968 with panels blown up huge.

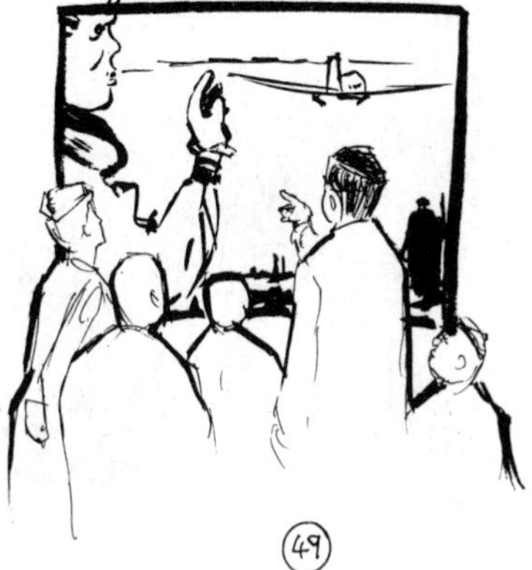

As a wee laddie of only fifteen, on your first time in London, you'll have stumbled on a book.

The Pop Art movement had put a spotlight on comics and it was inevitable that the history of the form would be reviewed and revised.

Lichtenstein, oil, 2ft high. 1961

Such things tend to be in the water a long time before bobbing to the surface.

The idea of artistic worth residing in the comics will have arisen naturally in the minds of some who made them and, more importantly, of a good number of the kids who read them

As a ten year old you could sort out all the different uncredited artists even when there was more than one fiddling about in the same pictures, which was the norm.

Far from it being a faceless industrial product, the comic book will have been to you a collective popular art not unlike jazz music used to be.

In a shop called *Bookends*, in a heady atmosphere of eclectica and esoterica, you will have discovered a remote shelf devoted to the literature that will have been growing around the subject.

Others will have been haunting this spot you probably pass them going in and out...

...each drawing from the implications his own conclusions, forming his own plan...

...to create a monumental kind of comic strip and add his own chapter to the story in these days when you will still have believed art to be a continuous narrative.

Between the French book and the *Penguin Book of Comics* by Perry and Aldridge and a whole slew of histories and collections that followed them onto that particular shelf in *Bookends of Camden*, you will have discovered the heroes of the next phase of your artistic life:

the grand old men of the newspaper comic strip: most of them dead by this time.

George Herriman

HEH?
Y'CAN GET A COUPLE OF PRETTY FAIR SODIES AT SCHNIEDERS' DRUG STORE FOR A DIME, JOE. WUTCHASAY?
Copyright, 1922, by Int'l

© King Features. 1922

Milton Caniff.

BUT I CAN'T TOUCH THAT GUN—I'M A CORRESPONDENT—A CIVILIAN!
MISTER, YOU'LL CORRESPOND TO A SIEVE IF YOU DON'T START POURIN' STEEL!

© Trib-News Syndicate. 1943.

Tad Dorgan

GANS

is Battling Nelson biting off more than he can chew

1906

Noel Sickles

ME PACK?—GEE I NEVER OWNED MORE'N ONE DRESS IN M' LIFE!—GIT YER GOGGLES ON FELLERS—TH' CINDERELLA O' TH' NORTH WOODS WANTS HER COACH!

OKAY!—THIS WAY, MILADY!—BUT IT'S A FLYING CARPET—AND WE'RE BOUND FOR BAGDAD ON THE SUBWAY—WHERE PRINCESSES GET IN AT TWELVE O'CLOCK—THE NEXT DAY!

© A.P. 1936.

Winsor McCay

I NEVER DID LIKE YOU!!!
THAT GOES BOTH WAYS! I WAS CRAZY WHEN I MARRIED YOU!

© N.Y. Herald. 1909

Clare Briggs.

YOU'RE ONE OF THE SLOWEST WORKERS I EVER SAW--MY ARMS ARE ABOUT READY TO BREAK

1926

Rube Goldberg.

IT'S A LONG TIME SINCE I HAD MY FACE MEASURED FOR A LAUGH

THAT'S ODD—A MAN LAUGHING IN BROOKLYN—HE MUST BE A STRANGER

THE INHABITANTS OF BROOKLYN SMILED FOR THE FIRST TIME IN SIXTEEN YEARS.

BROOKLYN, N.Y.

1919

Clift Sterrett
GUESS WHAT! MLLE. MODESTE HAS WROTE PAW A LETTER SAYIN' YOU AN' ME CAN'T HAVE ANY MORE CLOTHES TILL OUR BILL IS PAID!
GOOD NIGHT! DID HE HAVE A FIT?
© King Features.
1927
Roy Crane
WHY DO YOU TAKE THESE BACK ROADS INSTEAD OF THE HIGHWAYS, CHUCK?
OH.... YOU MISS THE CROWDS, AND THE SCENERY'S BETTER.
© King Features.
1956
John. Striebel
I HAVE SOME WONDERFUL NEWS!
1929
Harold Gray
CHARITY, EH- CHARITY!!! IF I WAS AS FULL OF CHARITY AS YOU ARE I'D BE THE MOST SUCCESSFUL MORTGAGE LOAN SHARK OUTSIDE OF SING SING-
© Trib-News Synd.
1924
Alex Kotsky
I'M SORRY... I MUST HAVE LOST IT!
1972
Fred Opper
FLENCHMEN VELLY HUNGLEE ME GETTEE 'EM SOME SOUP!
HELP! I FAMISH
I WISH TO RETURN INSTANTLY TO THAT DEAR PATERSON, N.J.
I STARVE
4
© King Features.
1906
Billy Debeck.
ALL OUR TROUBLES ARE OVER NOW, SWEET WOMAN - I GOTTA RACE HOSS!
SPARK PLUG
DEBECK
Copyright 1922
1922
Jimmy Swinnerton
7
OH, DE GLORY'S IN DE SKY! SING HO FO' DE LITTLE 'POSSUM!
© King Features.
1904
Stan Drake
GOOD NIGHT!
SLAM
GOOD NIGHT, GRADY.
© King Features.
1959

George McManus
WELL · SAY YOU SHOULD HAVE SEEN KID HEAD CHEESE KNOCK THE BLOCK OFF SLANT HEAD MORRIS LAST NIGHT · LOOK · HE STOOD LIKE THIS ·
©King Features.
1912
Elzie Segar.
LAUGH, EMMA, LAUGH!
I CAN'T SEE ANYTHING FUNNY ABOUT A MAN WITH HIS NOSE IN A VASE
11
©King Features.
1929
Walt Kelly
Honor Sick an' Davey Criss-Cross, MacTruloff said to me, Tutor Killduffs Anna Pottage inner Pair threes.
THAT'S HOW IT GOES... AN' NONE TOO SOON.
GIVE HIM A HAND... WHAT GOOD'S A PAIR OF THREES?
1967
Bud Fisher
YOU'RE A CLASSY LITTLE CHICKEN
FEEL HOW COLD MY HAND IS
THE PLACE
© King Feat.
1908
Frank King
THAT'S RIGHT, PAL, YOU'LL PROTECT ME, WON'T YOU!
GO AWAY PAL! I WANT TO BEAT HER UP.
© Trib-News Synd.
1929
Leonard Starr
... WHAT DID HARDING DO THAT WAS SO BAD ANYWAY?...
FORGET HIM. A LOT OF MEN VOTED FOR HIM TOO, WE HAVE A CONTEMPORARY PROBLEM... THERE'S SOMETHING WRONG WITH OUR ACCOUNTS...
© Trib-News Synd.
1968
R.F. Outcault.
1896
Jules Feiffer.
THIS PARTY IS FOR THE BIRDS. LET'S CUT OUT.
BRING OUR WINE BOTTLE. I HEAR ANOTHER ONE UPSTAIRS
8.
© Feiffer.
1956

Once the French guys get hold of a thing, it becomes in their essays a high and serious Art. They did this with the movies in their *Cahiers du Cinema* away back when.

So now it's the 'funnies'. Horn takes *Flash Gordon* (in his intro to one of the Nostalgia Press volumes) and compares and contrasts the 'drang und sturm' of Raymond's middle period with the classicism of his late, the panels ordered 'like French gardens'.

All of this kind of appeals to you at first and then one day you're looking back at Moliterni's dissection of Hogarth's narrative technique on *Tarzan*.

He's got "narrative technique" divided up into types, like 'parallel' and 'accelerated'. You decide it's all cuckoo and razor the pages out. I mean, *Tarzan*, I ask you!

Once you've done that, the book swiftly dismantles itself and you end up filing a couple of pages and losing the rest.

A remark of Henry Miller's in *The Air-Conditioned Nightmare* just about closes the matter. Seeing a 'funny sheet' on the ground while 'taking a promenade along the rim of the Grand Canyon' ('*Prince Valiant* was what caught my eye')

He writes: "What can possibly appear more futile, sterile and insignificant in the presence of such a vast and mysterious spectacle"?"

Anyway, all this will be running through your noggin while Claude's over there, sipping his Pernod.

You will be arguing with yourself that no matter where one's head has gone in the meantime, one should take the opportunity to acknowledge the receipt of influence at an earlier date and you will proceed forthwith:

He'll seem quite pleased to be recognized in a foreign place for a book published 16 years back.

The small, independent comics publishers are here, too; Knockabout, for instance, at this time right in the middle of another prosecution.

The police are trying an interesting new trick by getting them under the Obscenity law for books about drugs.

Attempt to widen obscene books act fails

The jury won't know what to make of it and the Knockabouts will go home happy but harrassed. They'll have just published a neat big fundraiser to cover legal costs.

They'll cheerfully get along like this forever. The tea-leaves show them fourteen years from here jumping out of an aeroplane to raise funds to fight an umpteenth prosecution.

The Escape boys are here, taking the opportunity to mooch an invitation to the big comics festival in Angoulême.

And the third English independent publisher, *Titan*, who will only ever put out collections of stuff that's already successful. Take chances, us?

If that's your mighty three-pronged cake-fork assault on the world of culture, you might as well go home and go to sleep. Wait! You've just seen Posy Simmonds hiding behind the rubber plant.

Her weekly half-page in *the Guardian* is a treasure.

How much I want to **spit** on your basket-weave!...
CRUNCH
CRUNCH
© Posy Simmonds 1984

Time to go. The Escape boys will have got what they want and will be slipping out just ahead of you.

wait. manners. Shake the host's mitt, mumble something in o-level French.

Moliterni's mitt will get in the way. You'll shake it again cheerily. You wouldn't have thought reading his book would be such a big deal. And you cutting it all up like that too.

Kiss the hostess in the French manner

It's been a wonderful time. I thank you, m'am

Then the Cultural Counsellor to the French Embassy's wife will say:

You must come again.

And you'll light out of there before anyone can contradict the sweet lady.

A good night's work.

A good night's work, indeed.

Noel Sickles - Scorchy Smith © 1935 - A.P. Syndicate

Addendum:
From Pat Rogers' editorial intro to *The Oxford Illustrated History of English Literature*, a must for us who don't mind a lot of pictorial documentation with our reading:

"Is literary history necessary? It is possible... to write great literature with little or no sense of one's place in a great tradition. Shakespeare would have had very little idea of his historical bearings. The truth is that literary history is a modern invention and so is the automatic sense which a modern writer must have of his location in the flow of literary time (whether or not he cares about it)."

Chapter Seven

The map of the history of Art is like any other map. There are main roads and side streets; old masters and lesser masters

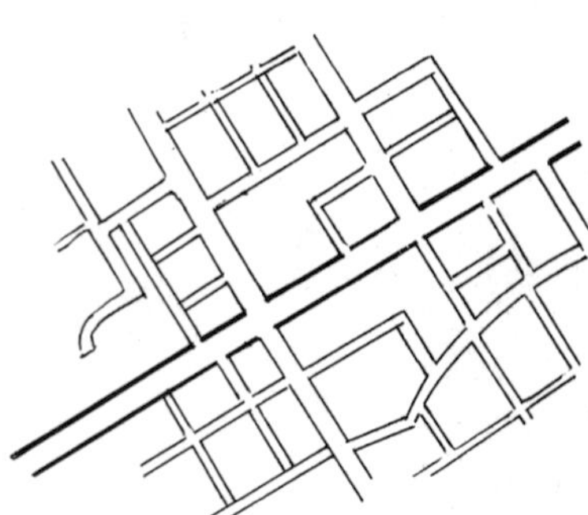

But there are also back yards, middens, coal bunkers and rhubarb patches; artisans so minor that their names will never be retrieved from the debris in the vacant lot.

Lovers of old art may speculate on whether the *Housebook Master* is the same bloke as the *Master of the Amsterdam Print-room* or whether the Circumcision in Aachen may be given to the *Master of the Tucher Altarpiece*.

No the fine things speak across physical and temporal distances. A song, a tale, a cartoon, a chair.

It may sound like moving old dust around to some, but the joy of spending time with those works is to you like a grand meal with a fine wine.

However, the pleasantly naive among us may think that the measure of art is that it "has passed the test of time". No map remains for long an accurate representation of the locale.

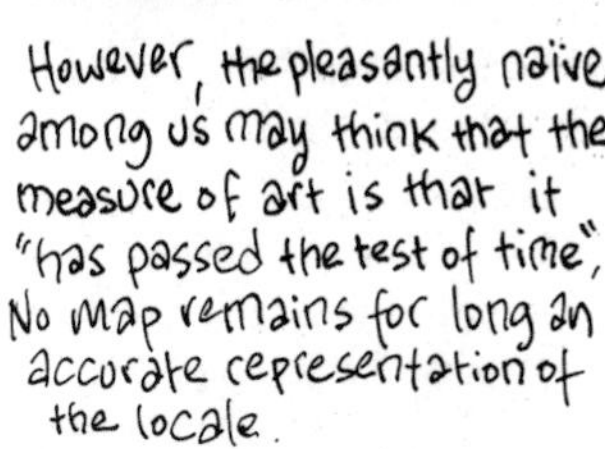

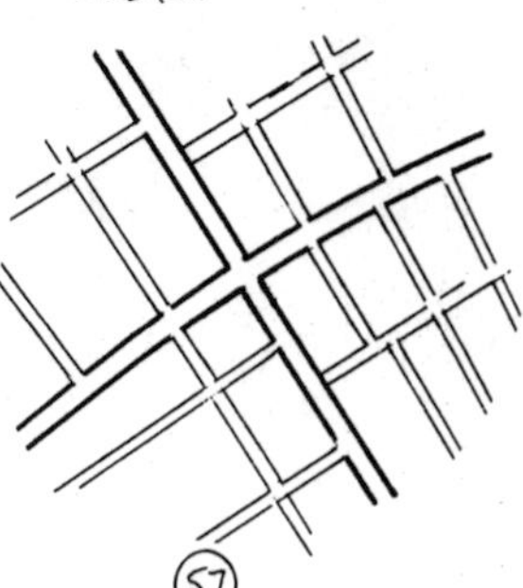

No doubt that's lost on many also. To them, eating and drinking is but refuelling. Keep a pump in the kitchen and top up three times a day.

Favour ebbs and flows. The crossroads is turned into a flyover, an underpass. The disused road was once a thoroughfare. The Via Roman underneath it all is nowhere indicated.

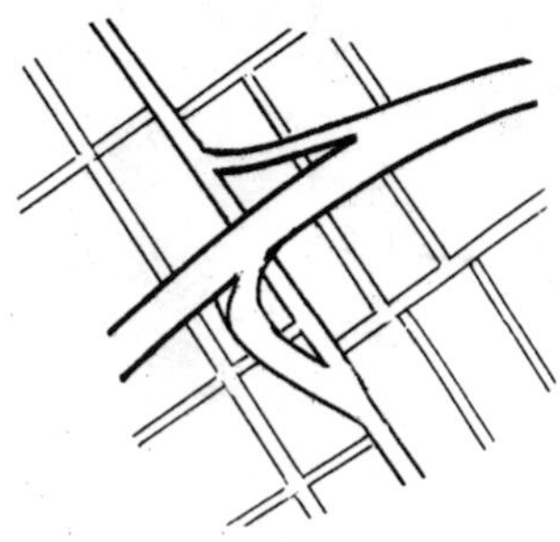

The 'academic' masters of the nineteenth century are getting attention again. There's a book on Gleyre, a painter so forgotten that of his 400 works in the musée Cantonal only one was on show, and that in a dimly lit corridor outside the main body of the museum when it was randomly destroyed by Vandalism in 1980.

Only the fragment of the weeping soldier remains of the execution of Major Davel.
1850

"I suspect the answer lies in our customary system of values which attributes merit to the Vanguard and relegates the rest to the heap of history". Another book presents itself; about the painter Meissonier, *The Plight of Emulation* (Gotlieb)

How come only now? One wonders at the fashion moving wholesale one way like that. Access roads closed. One way systems introduced.

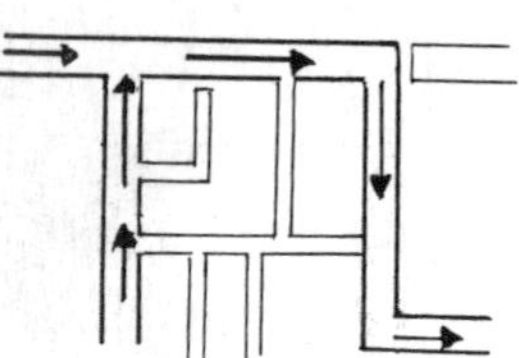

Those guys were always the villains, the 'traditionalists', pitted against the 'moderns' because the journalists of art like to say:

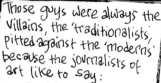

COME NOW, GENTLEMEN, LET'S YOU AND HIM FIGHT
segar, 1936 © King F.S.

Moderns Vs Traditionalists Art Vs Craft. The idea that art and craft are driving on opposite sides of the street is relatively new. It derives from another journalistic diversion, the myth of the Romantic artist-outsider. Like Van Gogh lopping his ear off-

Shelley at Lerici, aflame on the beach, age 29

Schubert in the looney bin, Age 31. The residue in the next century, the century of the neurosis of innovation, is "...a seemingly Romantic but in fact vague and hackneyed vocabulary of genius, imagination and artistic freedom"

(Gotlieb)

But we have become so inured to it that another book here on Gothic Art in Nuremburg feels it necessary to explain that back then not only were Art and Craft not seen as separate operations but "craft" was universally held in much higher esteem then.

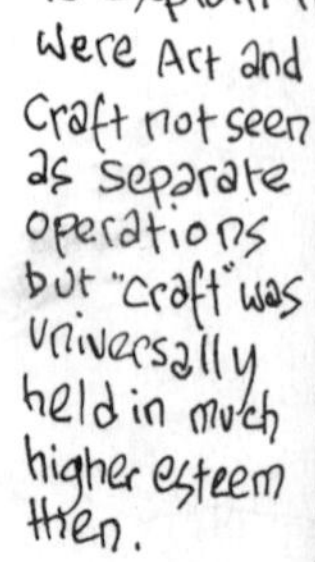

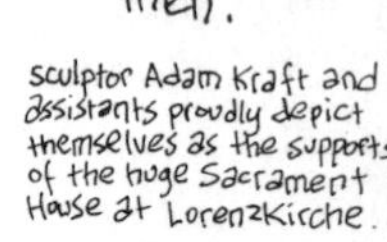

sculptor Adam Kraft and assistants proudly depict themselves as the supports of the huge Sacrament House at Lorenzkirche.

The same book, discussing the anonymity of 15th Century Masters, explains it as though we can no longer revive a tribal memory of how it used to be, even though anonymous works of art flicker past our gaze daily among TV commercials.

And it is careful to advise that just because an altarpiece happens to bear a master's signature doesn't mean he made the whole thing with his own two hands.

Strange that this has to be explained in a century when Disney signs all his movies and Ford signs all his autos.

The personal touch of the master. Another journalistic myth. They're everywhere.

RED! THERE!

The daydream is still in currency that one may labour obscurely in a garret in one's life and strut proudly down the mainstreet of the Map of Art in an artistic afterlife.

I would rather achieve immortality by not dying.

The adventure of fame is a separate one from the adventure of Art, though one may be used to further the other.

Self Portrait Warhol - 1970s

And Cartography is a separate discipline altogether: "This is the true spirit of history, which fulfils its real purpose in making men prudent and showing them how to live, apart from the pleasure it brings in presenting past events as if they were in the present" (Vasari, *Lives of the Artists* 1568)

Self portrait

The true history of humour may never be written. It defies that kind of organisation. It is the interlude, the relief, graffiti the half-hidden gesture, the barnacle, the midden, the rhubarb patch.

Print by Kuniyoshi: "Graffiti on a storehouse wall" - 1847, Japan.
(one presumes the artist is 'mugging' rather than reporting)

It's Shakespeare's clown, Will Kemp, Morris-dancing his way from London to Norwich as a stunt in 1600 and writing a book about it.

It takes you by surprise in reproductions from illuminated manuscripts. Sometimes it's ribald and obvious

Sometimes the subject isn't meant to be funny but you know from a certain feeling of kinship that the satirical monk got this job because the pious one had the flu that week.

Galen lecturing on the application of enemas.

It's in ancient Greek terracotta statuettes of everyday life.

Bosch

Chinese guy with bear on a pole.

a Japanese official

Images of lust and folly in obscure corners of medieval churches like these beard-pullers from France.

It's Sweet and gentle in Erasmus' *Praise of Folly*.

clap your hands, live well, and drink

Ms. Folly descends from the pulpit on the last page, from Hans Holbein's own hand-illustrated copy, c. 1515

It's vitriolic in the Reformation pamphlet war.

The Pope is crowned in the jaws of Hell c1545

English entertainer Charles Mathews in 1820's New York reported the following dialogue from a black production of *Hamlet*.

To be or not to be, dat is him question, whether him nobler in de mind to suffer or lift up him arms against one sea of hubble-bubble and by oppossum, end 'em.
Possum up a gum tree!
Possum up a gum tree
SING POSSUM
Possum up a gum tree

(CAST and audience break into song: POSSUM up a Gum tree, up he go, up he go)

Native American face-masks.

Iroquois, late 19th c.

It's Bernini's party-trick caricatures.

c 1640

It's banana skins.

Feet-ticklers.

the fart in the public library.

Chapter Eight

While some guy's jabbering about ART, you'll be moving house, Alec MacGarry.

It's the Australian, you see. They come from a big open place and they can never be happy again.

It's a country with nothing as far as the eye can see. You must go and see it for yourself (as an Australian once exhorted me to do).

Never one to waste time on these projects, you'll grab the first place you hear about

we've got to move out by the weekend.
Come again.
KILL

There will come a phase in your life when you move in and out of flats so fast you're already measuring them up for a nostalgic effect on your way in.

The landlady sports a sprig of broccoli in her front teeth. Surely she must notice.

It's an awful place. You'll sit on the front stoop and wonder what the hell you've gone and done.

The attraction was the Georgian bedroom doors big enough to drive a car through.

You'll hide all the godawful furniture behind the doors and install a couple of bean bags and one of those paper lightshades.

Now you'll be receiving guests any time you feel like it. Phoenix comes through the door like Tigger out of Winnie the Pooh.

The beds will be on castors and pass each other in the night till you think of removing the wheels.

No small wonder then that Annie announces the pregnancy.

The flat is in two parts, with the kitchen and bathroom set across the landing from the sitting- and bed room 2 keys.

Poor dearie will have to negotiate all this first thing in the morning.

Doesn't matter whether one's got 20 yards to run or 5, one still never makes the last two feet.

You'll still be working on the soldiers' files, putting them all on computer now.

One day you'll absent-mindedly make a correction with liquid white-out on the screen.

The gap between you and technology will only get bigger.

That same village-idiot quality elevates into an aroma of destiny that will surround you.
Perceptive individuals will see it, that holy haze about your head.
The colonel will offer you a lift in his big American Mercury. Nobody else has been thus singled out, apparently.
or whatever
What makes you do this job, Alec?
The job's for nitwits. You do it in two hours and spend the rest of the day writing.
The lesser lights among the management will get queer about that
Why's that man not working?
The colonel waves.
Good morning, Alec.
And a very good day to you sir.
And it's all so temporary The whole place is to be moved to Scotland in a year. They're phasing out the regular staff. Each one that leaves, in turn offers drinks.
It's drinks almost every Friday afternoon.
And then...
You wobble home with Chablis coming out your ears.
Good Night, Alec.
And a most wonderfully heartfelt good night to you sir.

Your brother, Mark, will arrive and occupy the spare bed over there by the curtains.

He'll spend the Summer intermittently selling cockles and mussels on Brighton seafront.

FRESH SEAFO

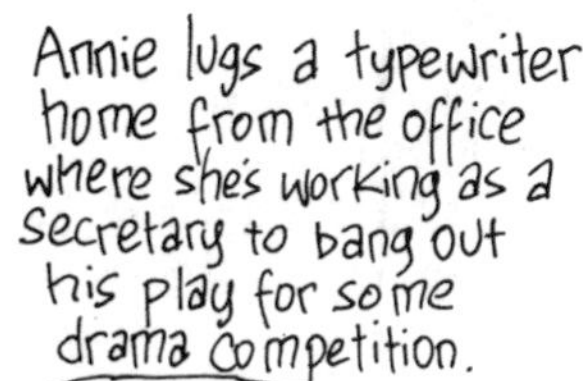

Annie lugs a typewriter home from the office where she's working as a secretary to bang out his play for some drama competition.

No, not SHIT
It's got to be S-H-I-T-E
What's the difference?

He's borrowing postage stamps and selling them on the Corner to make ends meet.

The space concept is brought up again

I need my space back.

Mark intercepts the landlady about the basement flat. She'll show it with a dog turd on the end of her shoe. Surely she must notice.

The sound of his clarinet rises into the night air till he has to sell it.

The bed has three legs. The mattress looks like the scene of a Ripper murder.

It was easier just feeding him; now you'll have to help him worry about his rent.

You'll draw into the wee hours, originality and skill in inverse proportion, as always, as everywhere, reaching towards the moment when they change places.

When are you coming to bed, honey?

On Sunday mornings there will often be a traveller on the spare bed over there by the curtains with holes big enough to pass a watermelon through.

Maybe tall Jenny from Canada.

Dakin with his guitar

Trevvy Trevs and Charmaine.

GOTCHA!

Everybody will be full of unfulfillable promise in the cheery winesodden Friday afternoon of your life when you feel an unbearable nostalgia for events less than a day after they happen. You just see if I'm not wrong, Alec MacGarry. Just see if the Monday morning of your life don't arrive like a broken elevator.

Letter from Phoenix. His visit to you will have galvanized him into dropping both the Town Planning course and the day job plan in exchange for being an artist complete and whole.

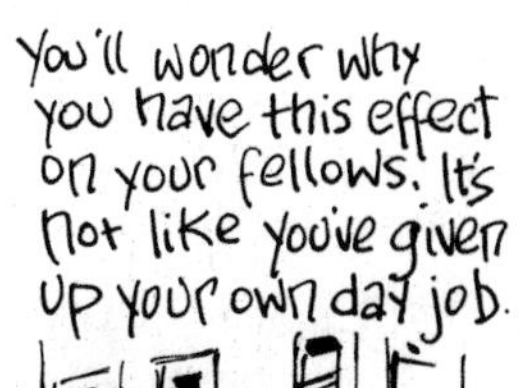

You'll wonder why you have this effect on your fellows. It's not like you've given up your own day job.

Elliott will have dropped his job right at the onset, just after you met him. Surely you wouldn't have known him long enough to be such a bad influence.

You'll take a holiday down to Devon with the Elliotts. Phil needs to have it all arranged in advance to allay all fears.

He's in convulsions of terror in case they misplace his booking and when he gets there nobody will know who he is.

GUEST HOUSE
We're all right

He cooks a midday meal and then enjoys his repose.

Now I'll have my scrumpy, dear.

You come up with a bunch of comic strip ideas to sell to "subject" magazines, like computer mags and medical journals etc.

HAVE YOU BEEN HAVING FLATULENCE?
WHAT DOES THAT MEAN?
OH NO...IT MUST HAVE BEEN ONE OF YOU!
(c) campbell - Elliott '85

Eventually you'll realize it's only keeping you both from your important work.

START WITHOUT ME
NOT FUNNY

The second part of your graphic novel will have come out a year after the first to hardly any notice whatsoever.

The 'media' thrives only on novelties, but you knew that, didn't you?

The trouble is; you'll feel that your second volume is definitely not as arresting as the first.

You'll determine to cure the problem with the opening to your third.

"A funny notion occurred to me while I was drowning..."
..."I saw humanity all pasted together with semen..."

The thing about hitting the mark with ideas is that you'll rarely know at the time when one has opened a door.

Usually you won't be aiming to kick a door in, just create a lively piece of humour

"It was dripping off the ends of noses."
Mother

One door's already banging in the wind. A comic called GAG lands in somebody's hands in California.

One of Elliott and Dakin's bright ideas, all the parties involved will have chucked in fifteen quid and got 200 copies to dispose of.

Letter from Dakin of six months back will be apposite.

Dear Alec
I am back in Dollis Hill after a week of restless drifting

-home, Liverpool and Manchester - actually looking back my wanderings ~~seem to~~ began when I visited Elliott in Maidstone - missing you and Anne by 20 minutes. Still, I managed to taste some of your Harrods Christmas pudding. Phil took me around on a heavily nostalgic autumn Sunday - pub by the river - it all seemed cosy compared with London.

Managed to pull !GAG! back on the rails even though I felt miles away from it in my heart. I don't want to be troubled by believing in it.

My head is ashy with comic thoughts - my fiery involvements of the last year have left a pile of comic ash and I don't care to reilluminate it.

Bit disappointed you didn't do a proper 'Alec' for !GAG!

I feel at the moment you are trying to peer above the 'small press' scene and advance - I don't blame you... It can be a trap - satisfying yourself artistically to a small press audience inevitably turns sour. You have to move on -

as far as I'm concerned the 'underground' scene has helped me regain enthusiasm and confidence - but just like Herriman, Segar, Caniff etc before us, we need that extra push to get into the 'big time' and hone sharp work for a wider audience.

Otherwise we will never get the full thrill from it all. The only problem is how to progress with dignity.

!GAG! : each party will have put most of his copies under the bed and forgotten about them. There will be no second issue.

Except the damn thing opens a door. I'm telling you this, Alec MacGARRY, so you won't muff it when it happens.

Stand on a high place and send out mental waves, subliminal messages

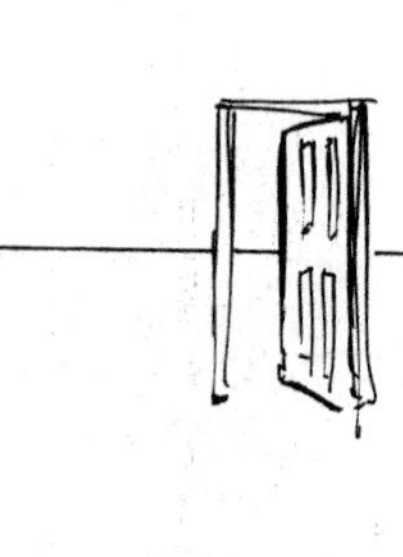

The doors will have been opening earlier than that, unknown to you. A few years from now when you eventually get to California...

You'll see one of those little photocopied booklets where Ilya helped you colour the covers, hanging up as a collectable for twenty times its original price, looking cosy in its 'mylar snug'.

Apparently Knockabout used them to pad the spaces in their shipping boxes going to the West Coast U.S.A.

Well I never

Draw the important stuff and lob it out there. Time will sort things out.

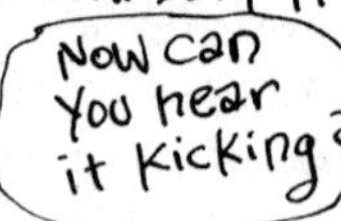
Now can you hear it kicking?

Chapter Nine

The first indication that serious critical acclaim is to visit the world of the comics will be Art Spiegelman's nomination for the National Book Critics Circle Award in biography for his *Maus*.

The first sign that there's any money in it will be Alan Moore's white suit.

New York is the center of this particular world. There will always be a center and you can depend on it being away over somewhere else. New Yorker Spiegelman imagined it would be France

Success will eventually demand of you an expedition.

Big hairy Alan Moore's stirring up a storm with the muck monster monthly so the company flies him into the Big Apple for a publicity jaunt. Safely back in Northampton, he gives Escape an article about it.

"I find I'm only able to sleep about 3 hours a night. There's an airconditioning unit which takes me two days to realise I can switch off and there is a little notice informing me that I should keep the door double-locked and always look through the peephole before answering in case it's a bag-lady with a meat cleaver and a shopping bag full of index fingers."

"Julie orders me a corned beef sandwich that consists of two slices of bread with a mound of beef between approximately the size of Mickey Rooney"

We'll all think he's joking and pay no attention to the signs, which include a narrative in *Knockabout* titled *Globetrotting for Agoraphobics*, which he'll get you to illustrate.

Moore's U.S. artistic collaborators on the muck monster, horror maniac Bissette, and Totleben, and their wives, will be over for the London convention.

Come and spend your last night with us and we'll get you to Gatwick airport.

At first they won't be too sure about it, but you'll get to play host with your big bedroom doors and assorted mattresses.

A million years from now when you own a house with more than two rooms you'll wonder at everyone enjoying this ramshackle hospitality.

As an afterthought, you'll show your Australian crime piece, *The Pyjama Girl*, or at least, the photocopy you had the sense to keep.

And in the morning Annie will drive you all around looking for an English castle

The best you can find is Roedean girls' school Bissette loves it.

MY GOD WHAT A CHILLY PLACE

You won't even be aware at the time of the importance of this friendship you'll have struck up.

Live well and toast the gods, Alec MacGarry. Fate is minding the wheel

The buzz that is in the air will be an intoxicating one.

Rumours will abound, get out of hand. The Americans mention the house which big hairy Alan Moore bought for his mother.

A house? That's not the way you will have heard it, from the man himself at the Westminster Arms.

It's nice not to have to worry, Alec...y'know, I've just bought me mum a greenhouse.
GUINNESS

A greenhouse. Not a green house.

And every time you'll see Americans incorrectly write "the green house effect", you'll picture wee Mrs. Moore tending her tomatoes.

Furthermore, for you, the expression will thereafter mean the way ordinary people tend to exaggerate the other guy's moderate success into an image of extraordinary wealth

Of course, from the small press, everybody else looks better off than yourself.

The difference between the guy who's on the right track and the one who isn't, is that the latter will begrudge a person their success

while the former will be quietly reassured in knowing that success is not such a faraway land.

Big hairy Alan Moore will be on the verge of becoming a celebrity.

Fate will move mountains to accommodate the man of destiny.
Ha! You mean even a slate falling off a roof will contrive to miss him?

He's already examining from a whole bunch of viewpoints the theme of a person's control of life and history in his first drafts of the script for the Watchmen, soon to be his first huge graphic novel success.

You'll be watching Danny Grey's alsatian having pups on a cold winter night. They're all coming out dead.

He'll have buried a couple before succeeding in getting the vet round.

The vet takes the third dead pup and does extraordinary violence to it.

Well, waddaye know? At times like this the difference between all and nothing can seem close to random.

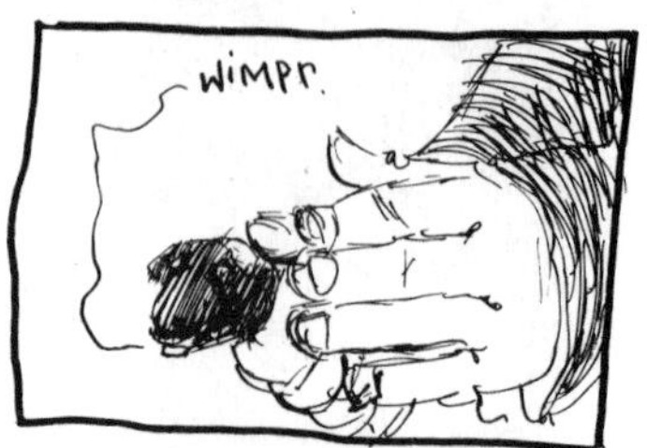

As an agent of Fate Danny Grey will find himself wanting. Make sure your account is in the black.

Alec, I think I killed the other two.

The reminders will be everywhere. Annie will slip on the ice, carrying the baby.

And you, carrying the new china dinner set. No damage.

In the collective noodle of history, or at least, that obscure corner of the car-boot of history where comics are remembered at all, it will be the age, or the phase, of the 'graphic novel'.

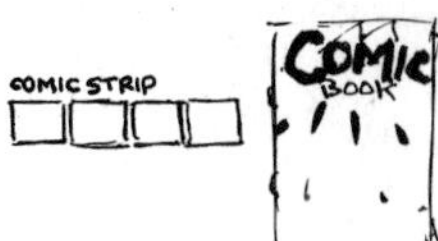

Really, all the man in the street will remember of comics will be the icons like Batman and Superman, Charlie Brown, Popeye.

But the bookish fraternity will have it divided up in phases, three in fact:
1. The newspaper comic-<u>strip</u>, which thrived in the first half of the 20th century,

HAW HAW!

But of course it was still around during:
2. The heyday of the comic <u>book</u>, the 40s and 50s, with occasional revivals after that.

And both survived to see the final great fireburst expiration of the art in its final phase, that of 3. the <u>graphic novel</u>.

"Graphic Novel". Will Eisner invented the term. He'd already had a career, as a young man, at the onset of the previous phase. You'll always get oddbodies that won't stay in their proper categories.

I'd like to show you something different... it's a... uh... novel. You might say a, uh... graphic novel...
BANTAM BOOKS

A Contract With God, in 1978, was the book. The idea of a big damn serious event of a comic dealing with stuff worth thinking and talking about was already fermenting in various heads:

This isn't quite it, but who'd've thought Eisner..

Of his next two, appearing in parts over the following eight years, *Life on Another Planet* will seem a step backwards but *A Life Force* will be the goods.

YOU HAVEN'T CHANGED AT ALL! I RECOGNIZED YOU AT ONCE..
OH, JACOB, I'M AN OLD LADY NOW!

'85 © Will Eisner. *A Life Force*

There can be displays of sentimentality and melodrama in Eisner's 'serious' works that would be at home in a reconstruction of Dickens but sit uncomfortably in the 1980s. However his best book waits down the track...

So he invented it and then it got hijacked by the moneyspiders and the bullshitters issuing their foolish masquerades as 'graphic novels' so that we'd just as soon go back to calling the real McCoy just 'comics'

It wasn't clear when Moore's first significant big work was coming out in parts in Warrior that it was a 'graphic novel'. Far from the 'center', it got lost in the confusion of publisher-collapse and acrimony.

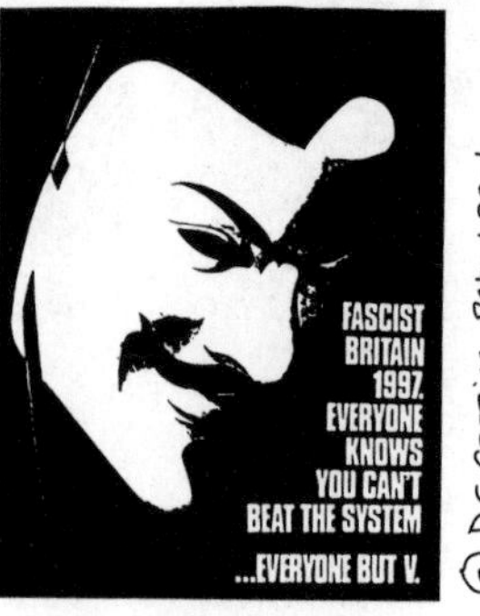

FASCIST BRITAIN 1997. EVERYONE KNOWS YOU CAN'T BEAT THE SYSTEM
...EVERYONE BUT V.

© D.C. Comics. Art: Leach.

And it won't get finished until after his second big work will be a roaring success.

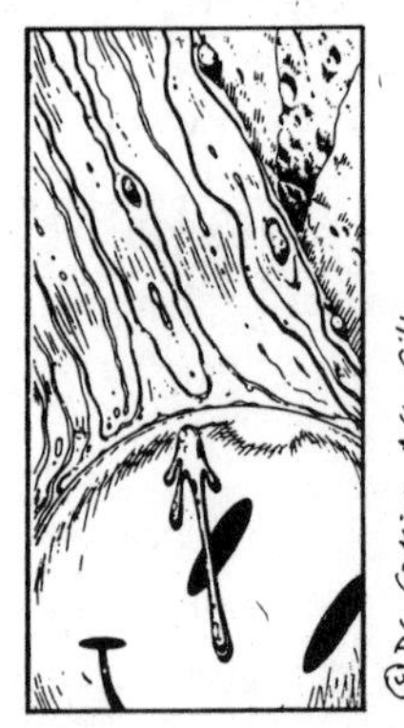

© D.C. Comics. Art: Gibbons.

In between these he churns out the muck monster for four years. The graphic novel is the mountain peak on a solid core of bread and butter.

TYPITTY TYPE TYPITTY TYPE

Comicbook scribblers will become fashion plates

HAVE YOU SEEN BILLY THE SINK ?

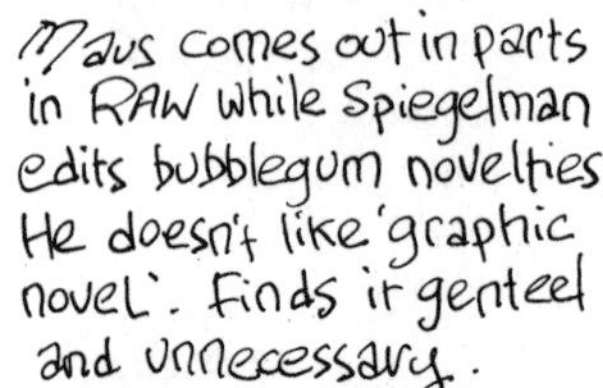

Maus comes out in parts in RAW while Spiegelman edits bubblegum novelties. He doesn't like 'graphic novel'. Finds it genteel and unnecessary.

YOU WILL TAKE AN UNEXPECTED TRIP!
DOWN A MANHOLE!

© Topps Bubblegum. Art: Lynch.

The media will be gathering on the phone wires.

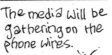

1986. It's funny how a whole mess of things will happen all at once.

Alec! My waters have broken
oh Jeezis oh fuck oh.

The first time you go through this you will be certain it's Fate testing you.
Here! More GAS
GAAHH
You'll be just thinking of yourself as usual, but God knows what women are really thinking at this moment.
Get a GUN! Shoot me and your bloody self
So now you'll be a big daddy, Alec MacGarry.
You'll lie awake at night listening to her breathing.
Then you'll imagine she's stopped.
You'll feel that you have connived your way into a job for which you're not qualified.
what if you're found out?
QUICK! the baby!
You'll have inherited a cot and pram and stuff from the Elliotts.
They'll have decided they're not going through all that again, and they never do.

Annie's parents will be staying at the time the baby arrives.

Her dad will be waiting outside the Cricketers for you every night on your way home from the office.

One night you'll forget to go home for dinner

He's the shire Chairman of the County of Hinchinbrook in tropical North Queensland which is like the country version of the mayor.

He'll come armed with a document of introduction with which to present himself to British dignitaries.

Meeting no dignitaries he'll give it to the barman of the Cricketers

you're the only important person i've met so far
Gee

Then they'll fly off leaving behind them a bad case of homesickness

That's all you need

Chapter Ten

Fate taketh and Fate giveth away

A month after becoming a father you'll finish your day-job. You won't know it then, of course, but it's the last one you'll ever have.

That won't be so bad; it's on the cards. But the very same day you'll lose your art job, the weekly *SOUNDS* thing

"For some time I've had misgivings about your strip cartoon...

Exactly one night later there'll be a foreign voice asking if you were to be invited on an all-expenses paid trip to Switzerland, would you accept?

You have to go, darling; don't worry about me

The man at the Crossroads will explain:

It's the comics festival in the little Alpine town of *Sierre*. Each year they have a different guest country. Last year it was China, next it's India. I'm coming with you, at my own expense.

So a committee of people in the know will have selected five representatives of British Comic Art, to show the broadest spectrum, and you'll be in it, for your isolated and ambitious use of autobiography.

You'll think it odd, being wined and dined in the Alps at a time when you're completely out of work, but these things are to be expected. Trust me.

Tell you what though; you never realized they got 40° heat up there.

Brian Bolland's another invitee. You first knew him 12 years ago during your wasted year at Art School in London.

It's a pity we don't meet these days, Alec. We seem to be in separate camps.

He'll have been the first in a growing wave of British talent moving in on American comic books, a phenomenon he represents like this:

cover Comics Journal 1987 © BOLLAND
retouched from the colour by Campbell

Kevin O'Neill's here too. He's an agreeable oddity. with writer Pat Mills he does a thing full of the wicked satire of a rejected Catholic upbringing.

© IPC 1981 - Nemesis by Mills e O'Neil

We're met in Geneva by an expat Liverpudlian named Gordon and it's up into the Tobleroney Alps...

...Always another one behind the one you see.

Fendant and *dôle* wines at a street-table café all paid for by the festival. You're concerned on behalf of the show about their money being chucked about so merrily. Maybe you should get out more often, Alec MacGarry.

hey, you're the guest.

You'll never have the run of an expense account like that. and will remain unsure as to whether you enjoy being on either side of this indirect line to the owners money.

I've been escorting Don Lawrence and his wife around for 2 days. this is nothing

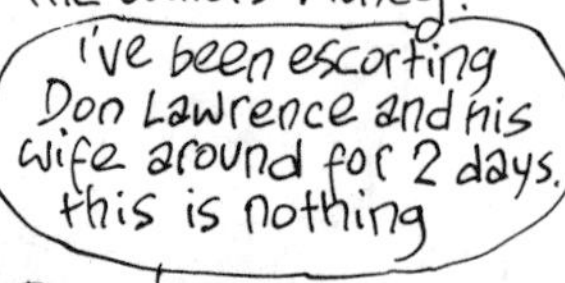

Gordon's a volunteer at the festival, immediately assigned to *British liaison*. His own work is his small bar in the hills, a tourist thing. In the off-season (now) he buys up novelties to sell:

such as ski-poles with hollowed hand-grips to hold a few nips of cognac

also, I'm importing this thing called a 'reflex'

a what?

It's a flat light-box kind of thing with some kind of fluorescent gas in it but with an opaque black coating...

...which, when stroked with special waxy coloured crayons registers and holds a brilliant luminous line.

You won't know what the hell he's talking about and you'll put it to the back of your noodle for the moment. Sierre is a pretty little town, with a main street, in a deep Alpine Valley.

Outside the *Hotel Terminus* there's wee funny Hunt Emerson, and Don Lawrence, making the five. Colin Wilson's here too. A New Zealander, he landed in the U.K. five years earlier but was not permitted to stay. Moved to Belgium where he'll spend the choicest part of his creative life drawing the young version of somebody else's character. Quite happily, no doubt. The things you have to do to be an artist.

You and the *Man at the Crossroads* will be in the hotel next door for the first night. You've got a room with no shower. Doesn't matter. This is the last you'll see of it.

Dinner in a big marquee. It's starting to rain. A little band playing Swiss music comes across the lake on a raft

You'll watch Hunt disintegrate his quiche to remove the ham. Roast beef and ratatouille follows. He manages to get a double helping of the latter without any of the former.

In a bar, later, there's almost a punch-up.

Two young wankers are trying to wind you up. Don Lawrence stops you from mixing it.

come away, Alec - You've got no Health insurance here.

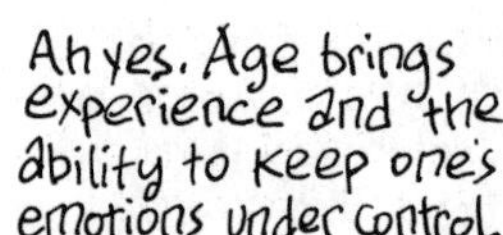

Ah yes. Age brings experience and the ability to keep one's emotions under control.

Don's an English comics artist from way back, now doing all his work for a Dutch publisher. There's a whole generation of artists in this business with a heap of disgruntlement from being ripped off by the business people.

I KNOW WHERE TO GET MILLIONS OF CREDITS...
... BUT IT WILL TAKE TIME!
STORM by LAWRENCE © '80

That's an inevitable side of Art. It's not necessarily in the artistic temperament to be good at business or to care to think about it, so there's potential in the business department for taking advantage of the situation.

Over the next few days, sitting near Lawrence doing signings, you'll notice he always does his sketches in pencil and if possible on a coloured endpaper.

dédicace?
JE DETESTE LE TRAVAIL

Makes reproduction more difficult, you see. But you won't make this observation till later, till after the events of the final night.

ah, yes.

You're locked out of the hotel. This won't strike you as unusual till you've travelled a bit more in your life. Don throws a stone at a window where it happens Hunt can't get to sleep.

Here's a picture of Hunt asleep, by himself, though actually he'll have brought his sweetie along on this trip.

©81 Emerson by Emerson

As for you, you're sleeping with an Alsatian dog in Gordon's mountain chalet.

You wake up on the mountain and you're supposed to be in the valley.

They're hanging about outside the hotel when you get there, with Nadine and Benedicte who are looking after us.

You're back in the original hotel Crossroads has put your unopened suitcase in your room. This is the first time you've seen an electronic key. You have to get someone up to open the door for you. But there's still no shower. Use the one in the corridor.

You're too late for breakfast. You order a cappuccino, which Gordon indicates is to be put on the slate.

Now here's the British exhibit at the town hall. 38 current artists represented. A fine coming together of the various denominations of the comics scene.

Old pros like Embleton and Lawrence next to new-wavey photocopy guys like Flewitt and Pinsent, even newspapery stuff like Posy Simmonds. and there's that daft bugger Alec MacGarry, still asleep at the turnpike.

In the next gallery, a sampling of Dennis Gifford's collection of old British original art pages. Gifford's here too to make sure nobody spills anything on them.

Gifford will have had a number of posh-looking books out from various publishers. They're mainly an excuse to show the world his prodigious collection of old comics.

An artist himself, his claim to fame was the *Classics Illustrated Baron Munchausen*, created for the English editions and the only one ever done in a cartoony style.

It's a funny old world, the world of arT (with a capital T). In its back alleys you'll find all kinds of old junk dropped out of windows.

And speaking of junk, in the Town Hall the president of the festival has had a signing area done up in a way he considers 'English', which is to say, like Madame Tussaud's.

There's a lump of turf he had the presence of mind to lift from Hyde Park, and a very grey looking flag, but not the one from the Charge of *the Light Brigade* which looks more like a fishing net now and hangs in St Paul's.

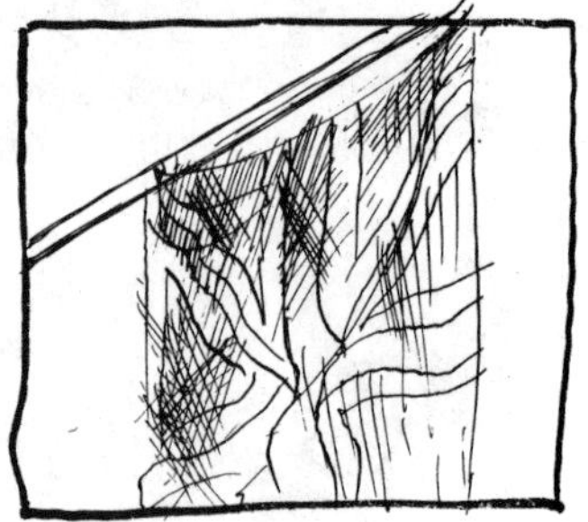

At some point over the weekend Hunt mops up a beer with it.

The main marquee's alive. All the European publishers are arranged neatly with their latest "albums" advantageously displayed. None of your jumble sale British comic marts here.

It puts us all in perspective, eh?

You're here for the local T.V. *The Man at the Crossroads* does all the translating, but it's a shambles. The fact is, MacGarry, you won't be crossing that language barrier now or later.

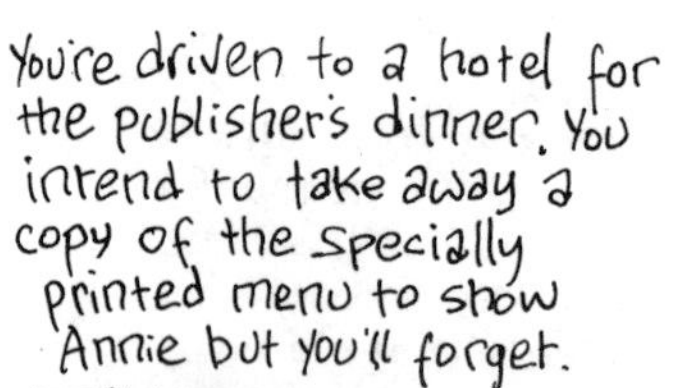

You're driven to a hotel for the publisher's dinner. You intend to take away a copy of the specially printed menu to show Annie but you'll forget.

It's chicken breast with a vegetable stuffing. You wonder what Hunt's going to do to it.

Later, in a bar, there's one of those damn "reflexes" on the wall. So that's what it looks like. Gordon's all shitty because he's the only guy in town who's got them and he didn't sell this one.

He phones the copshop to ascertain whether his lock-up's been broken into. It has. He has to leave.

In the hotel it's too hot to sleep. You shake the quilt down to the end of the bag and sleep under the empty bit.

Actually, the reason you can't sleep is that Nadine slipped you a note saying to meet Hugo Pratt at ten at the info desk. You still have the note. You didn't dream it.

You're so distracted you forget to take your key out to the shower and end up wet at the front desk.

You get down in time for breakfast. Gifford's whingeing about how you can only get breakfast coffee at breakfast. After that it's cappuccino or espresso

Well, you have to mention that you're meeting Hugo. News like that you just can't keep to yourself

I knew him in London 20 years ago. It would be nice to see him again.
You can help me recognise him

It's like that scene in Laurel and Hardy where "There's gonna be a fight"

Oh, can I come.
I could tape an interview for Escape

I've always wanted to meet Hugo

Majestic Hugo Pratt is one of the few famous people you'll meet who won't fail to impress. From Italy to Ethiopia to Argentina to England to France to Switzerland. Author of *Corto Maltese*.

JAVA, SEND THIS TO MILNER THE LAWYER.

Hugo Pratt - '70 © Casterman - Corto Maltese

Gifford will get him talking about the old days and Crossroads will tape it. Presumably nothing great will be said because you will not notice the chat published anywhere, so we're reading some words from an older interview with the mighty fellow who will no longer be with us when this document goes public

I once wrote a kind of an autobiography where I talked about people, and through them, about myself. Everyone said it was a wonderfully funny autobiography.

Whereas I thought I'd written a very sad book. Scary, in fact. It was the end of my youth, the evocation of people who have died, who have disappeared. No one noticed the poetic touches.

Corto Maltese.

You'll have to go and do a signing at the Town Hall and it will occur to you that you never discovered what Hugo wanted to see you about

uh... dedicass ?

But later that day, you'll be passing the exhibits, running late for another scheduled event and there will be Hugo, with the Man at the Crossroads talking up a storm. They're standing before your own work

You'll pass just close enough to hear Hugo ask a question:

Tell me, how does he do that with the little dots?

Lovely Switzerland with its cheese salads and cowbells in the mountains. There's Somebody tumbling out of a doorway here.

Don Lawrence is doing an appearance on a German-Swiss Television channel.

The M.C. kicks off with a leading question: Isn't it odd, a wee hick town like Sierre trying to do a big International festival (roughly translated)

Don declines to discuss his hosts in such terms. A French-Swiss butts in on his behalf.

The big German-Swiss pops the little French-Swiss on the beak. Don tries to break it up but he's all wired for sound.

Ah, yes. One day, when you're older, Alec MacGarry, you'll be so cool as to break up other people's fights and not get into any of your own.

Later, a girl will ask Don to do a sketch on her back, which gives the Reuter's photog. an idea.

He'll find a willing pretty girl and with Lawrence and Emerson and Gifford you'll cover her with cartoon characters. It'll go out on the wire. You might find it in your local paper.

You worked with Don Lawrence!? What on?
A young lady's back.

Now it's dinner in the Chateau de Venthône. (13th Century)

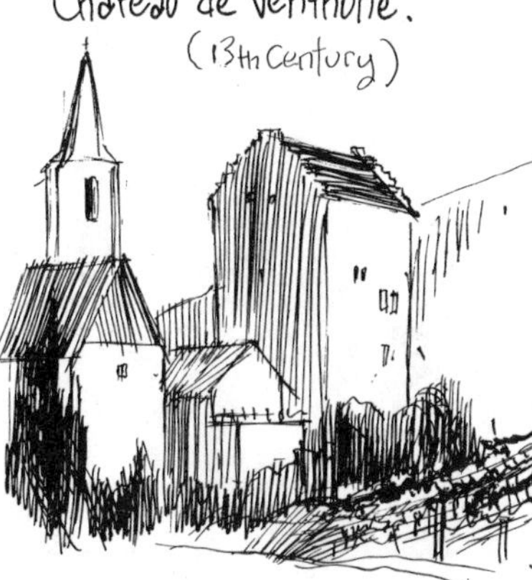

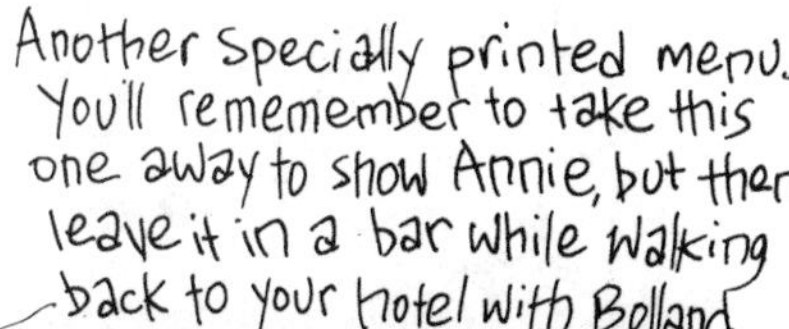

Another Specially printed menu. You'll rememember to take this one away to show Annie, but then leave it in a bar while walking back to your hotel with Bolland.

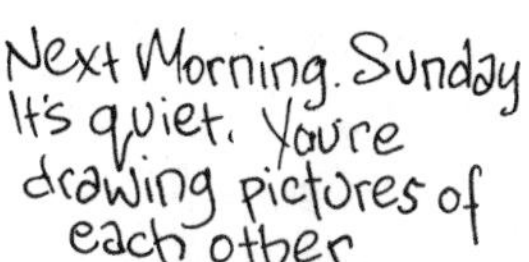

Next Morning. Sunday. It's quiet. You're drawing pictures of each other.

HUNT EMERSON= Siere BD86.

A lot of guys in this game have their own little worked-out presentation sketch which they repeat every time but Hunt always creates one anew...

Spinning out his improvisations like a jazz soloist.

The whole show closes down and beer and wine appear. We're doing sketches all the way back up the street for people who've just managed to get out of bed.

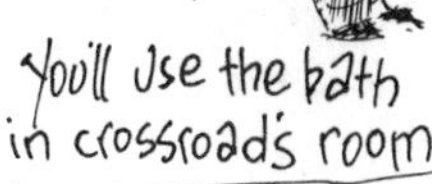

You'll use the bath in crossroad's room.

Then all the takings will be spent on a slap-up meal, which is a bummer. You'd kind of hoped to take some home,

The wine'll be all kind of bitter everywhere you go, all Fendant and dôle. You'll have a word with Gordon and he'll phone ahead to another place to put some Muscat in the chiller.

You'll read somewhere that *Muscat* is the only grape that when vinified still tastes like grapes. What an astonishing thought.

You thought there was just red, white and Thompson Seedless. You make a mental note to investigate this wine thing at greater length. There's obviously a lot more to it

Anyway we arrive at Café *Muscat*, and the denouement of this adventure.

Here's Ash. I've been saving him till now. He's Nadine's husband; one of those blokes that seeks to impress by doing psychological analyses of everyone present.

Hunt, you're a small fellow. You got by as a child by making everybody laugh. The camera is turned upon you and you feel obliged to be funny.

Don is hiding in fantasy. But his feelings are tempestuous, and not too far under the surface

My own story is very interesting and one day I shall tell it. Now there's a thought. Nobody is doing their own experiences in comics.

well actually thats what Alec's doing

Truly? what do you do when you catch up to today? Do you run out of material?

ARGGH. WHAT A HORRID THOUGHT! That my life's work should end here with me listening to HIM... Gotta get away—

Now, Gordon will be in the middle of selling one of his Reflex things to the landlord. He must have brought it in the boot of his car.

A splendid notion forms itself in your bean and you call Hunt over.

Well, naturally, he improvises a bit of business without needing to be asked.

And then everybody's adding to it; Don, Bolland, Barrie, Arthur, O'Neill, Jewelz. It's quite a collectable object

picture it on your mantelpiece.

Meanwhile, Ash is still psychoanalyzing. The bitter wine is obviously less dense than the sweet because it's coming to the surface, all acidity and sucked-in cheeks.

Apparently Ash and Nadine got sacked by the festival for going way over budget in the U.K. department. But to his annoyance, silver-tongued Gordon came out of it smelling of roses.

Splutter

(yes, laugh you may)

So now he's poisoning Don's ear with an analysis of Gordon.

He's a hustler and a con-man. You wait and see. He'll be selling his Reflexes with your pictures reproduced on them, profiting from your work

The night's finishing. Going out you see the Reflex. But all the graphic delights have been erased.

It's Don. He's waiting outside the door for Gordon to appear so he can punch his lights out. Ah yes.

Don't wipe it!

For God's sake man, the things are worth more without our drunken scribbles all over them.

get your facts right Alec.

It ends in a shouting match. Oh well, at least you wiped the inflammatory remark. Written offence is harder to forget than alcoholic ranting on the morning after.

People are funny monkeys. Morning: You've left your toothbrush in Crossroads' room.

You'll phone Gordon and he'll come down with the big alsatian dog. Everybody makes up over breakfast. The president of the festival gets train tickets sorted.

Thanks for wiping that, Alec.
HA! I owed you one

Geneva

ENTHUSIASM
ENTHUSIASM
ENTHUSIASM

London

I have a sudden desire to eat some leeks.
I think we may have some in the fridge.

Brighton

I'm ho 2ome
What in God's name have you been eating?

Chapter Eleven

You're down off the mountain, Alec MacGarry. Now what do you do?

On top of the world one day, fretting about money the next. But it's not like things aren't developing fast...

The Man at the Crossroads will call you up to London to help present a slide-show and talk at the Royal College of Art.

...to accompany a small exhibition of the new comics in the cafeteria organized by small press man Caspar Williams.

Elliott will be there too but will vapourize just before going in.

Hey, where's Phil?
Whaddaya know - He's gone again.
You mean he's done this before?

AARG

That'll be just one of Crossroads' endeavours. Between that and publishing *Escape* magazine and its offshoots (including your books, Alec MacGarry), he'll be writing articles for mags all over the place on the subject of "the new comics".

He'll be ruling connecting lines across a firmament of artists, from the hip Hernandez brothers in California.

WE STUMBLED AROUND SMALL TALK. SHE SEEMED REALLY IMPRESSED WITH MY, ER, ACADEMIC STANDING, EVEN IF SHE KEPT FORGETTING MY NAME. BUT I WAS USED TO THAT.

© Beto Hernandez '85

To the surreal Bob Burden in Georgia.

Peter Pronto

© Bob Burden '84

The mad and sensitive visions of Chester Brown in Canada.

© Chester Brown © 85

The acute ear of Susan Catherine in Seattle.

"Trudy got her body down to nothing but it still looks like she's storing nuts in those cheeks."

© Susan Catherine '86.

Pekar in Cleveland, the original autobiographer, who on the wave of comic book popularity finds himself on the David Letterman show and returns for two rematches.

© Harvey Pekar '87

The older Raymond Briggs, Children's-book illustrator in England, arrives at the graphic novel from a different angle from the rest of us, and sticks with the form. His *When the Wind Blows* of '82 is made into a celebrated animated movie.

© Raymond Briggs '82

It's not often that a coherent movement springs up spontaneously in a lot of different countries like this. Crossroads will introduce you to the work of Lat, of Malaysia.

The media is suddenly interested; Crossroads will expand his pieces out of the afficionado publications like *Cahiers de la Bande Dessinée* into art journals like *Illustrators*

and then to full-blown colour pieces for news-stand youth and style magazines; 6 pages in Jamming, 11 in I-D magazine

© Lat. '87.

Other journalists will get into the act and the whole thing will snowball. For a season comics will be the popular story.

From the tabloids to the culture pages of *The Times* and the *Observer*.

Roger Sabin will be one of that wave of journalists. He'll later write a book about the phenomenon: "The barriers between high and low culture were, if not breaking down, then leaking badly."

Sun, TimeOut, NME, Sunday Telegraph, NME

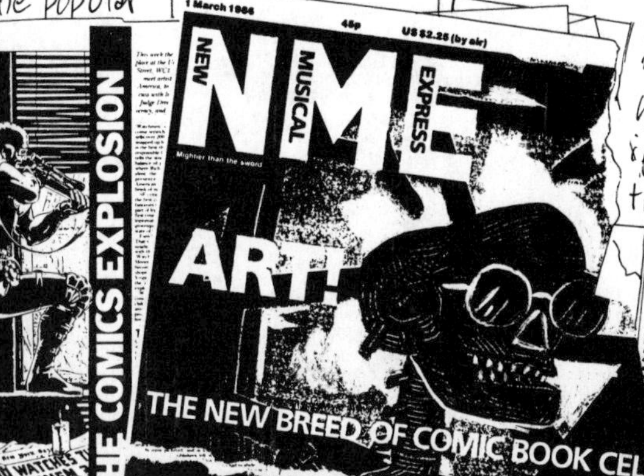

© Sheehy - Harper-Collins '95

"London in the Spring of 1986, when it seemed like everyone was swilling champagne and the girls wore mini-skirts and the men drove classic cars."

...And they all had graphic novels on their coffee tables. Ah, but you're fated to be ever out of step with your times, Alec MacGarry.

Here comes big hairy Alan Moore for a visit, fresh and vibrant in the shine of the *Watchmen's* successful arrival. 3 of the 12 parts are out.

And with him, his 'extended family', comprising his wife, Phyllis, their two kids and then her 'girlfriend', Debbie.

The delicate matter of sleeping arrangements:

HOW MANY PEOPLE CAN WE GET ON THIS MATTRESS?
THREE

The Watchmen by Alan Moore and Dave Gibbons will be one of the successes of the season, with the 12 parts wrapped up by mid '87 and the whole then issued in a single 500 page volume.

© D.C comics '87. Moore-Gibbons.

Batman. Well, of course, the whole plot has already gone to fuck as you can see right there. But it's too late. It's in the hands of the PR Yuppies

© DC Comics. Miller

Techically American in origin, all three will be on the best seller lists on both sides of the Atlantic, *Dark Knight* in Britain for as long as 40 weeks.

Frank Miller, left, is th
American artist whose
"graphic novel" sold
millions. Now, ROB RY
reveals, Fleetway's cha
could bring British stri
US-style status at home

IMAGINE Ian Fleming, having written Casino Royale, being told by the publisher that he did not own his James Bond character; furthermo Bond could be given

portrayed in the stri
In June this
Baxendale finally
future re-prints, film rights or merchandising deals.
Unlikely? In the book world perhaps, but practices such as

Observer Dec '87

The other two, for the media will eagerly boil it down to "THE BIG THREE" will be *Maus*, the first half of it out as a 160 page book.

PUT ASIDE ALL YOUR PRECONCEPTIONS.
THIS IS NO TOM AND JERRY CARTOON.
THIS IS A NEW KIND OF LITERATURE.

A SURVIVOR'S TALE
Now in paperback

Penguin Books

© 86. Spiegelman

The Watchmen and *The Dark Knight* will both be published in British editions by Titan. They'll get in a whiz kid named Igor Goldkind.

"There was a marketing opportunity. My job was to develop a semantic the general public and the book trade could understand."

Moore will be a celebrity, his white suit everywhere.

THE OBSERVER

WEEKEND

Shazam! The hero breaks down

The neurotic super-hero has arrived. Today's comics, writes DON WATSON, deal with real problems.

observer. '87.

And *The Dark Knight*, Frank Miller's dramatic revision of Batman, 4 48-page parts collected.

© D.C Comics '87. Miller.

"Literature for the post-literate generation" will be one of the phrases befuddling our ears.

Watchmen. Moore-Gibbons © DC.

The comics companies are collecting every old nonsense from their published inventories into "graphic novels". Nevertheless it's possible to trace a line of progress. Take *Violent Cases* by Neil Gaiman and Dave McKean,

© Gaiman-McKean. Escape-Titan Nov '87

Gaiman will be the most perceptive of the journalists arriving on the scene in '86; will write some articles on comics, including a review of the third Alec yearly part in Knave magazine —

Will host a panel with Moore and Gibbons at the '86 London convention.

© Campbell. Escape '86

And with McKean will talk on his own account on an '87 TV production which will also have Myra and Gibbons.

It's an incredibly exciting time to be in comics.

Spiegelman, with the critical success of *Maus*, resents giving up his career as an artist for one as an interview subject

is the recipient of a Guggenheim award and gets back to work on the second half of his masterpiece. He starts by reflecting upon the horrors of public attention that followed the publication of the first half.

© Spiegelman '88

Published in parts for six years by Spiegelman in *RAW*, Maus goes with Random House for the 'book market'. (PENGUIN IN THE U.K.)

So now all the "book" publishers will want a piece of the pie. Kyle Baker's experience is not untypical:

around the time the *Dark Knight* and *Maus* came out in the book market, Doubleday thought that comics would be the next big thing, so they published any cartoons they could find. I said I had some.

With no "reservoir" the book companies will have to cast about and commission new works. Alas, foolish novelties will be the order of the day. Or is that just a bunch of sour grapes, Alec MacGarry?

And that's where it will fall apart. Most of the people making the decisions will not have any real grasp of the situation. But it will be a mad couple of years for those caught in it.

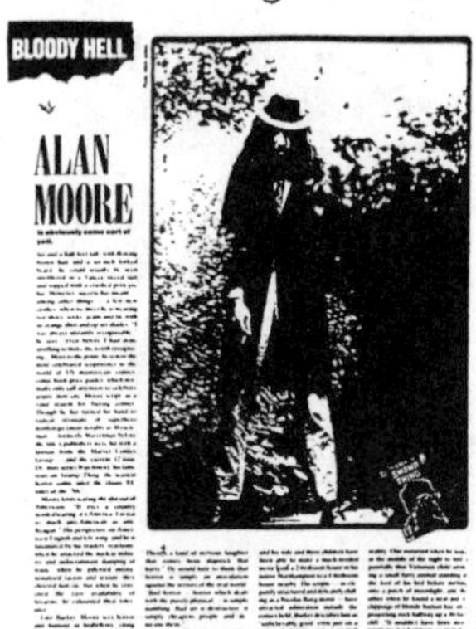

© Q magazine. Oct '86

Chapter Twelve

Alec MacGARRY, don't go saying yes to the emotional demands of a woman in the afterwash of childbirth. No! Don't!

I want to go home to Australia and if you don't want to come I'm going anyway.
say ma ma ma ma
blg
well... I guess there's no champagne or classic cars keeping me here.

Too late. Oh well, at least you'll have a plan. A plan of compromise.

It'll be four years since you danced out of the pointless dead-end job.

That won't seem a long time to cling to an ideal in retrospect, in the way that Odysseus' nineteen years away from Ithaca, while Penelope waits for him, seem impossible to to a young bloke but not so to an old one.

The plan: an improbable success in the States, titled *The Teenage Mutant Ninja Turtles* will have opened up a lucrative oportunity for enthusiatic amateurish comics. Elliott is the first in.

I just got advance orders of 13,000. You should give it a try too.

All kinds of successes will be published out of back bedrooms, looking cheap as blazes.

It's too easy. I'll make a bundle.

The hypothesis of the intelligent comic book novel is accepted and then the next dog out of the traps is a wave of daft juvenilia.

GOT ANY BEER?
© Eastman + Laird '85

So you'll need money and come up with some badly drawn American-style comic-books. Don't worry. The world will forget.

Meanwhile, the life you lead inside your head will follow its own course.

You keep all your cuttings and correspondence in loose leaf files

That way you change the order of it. Reshuffle it, extend a branch, prune another. History shapes up differently every time.

The artist is given a different role in each version. Sometimes he fails his own audition altogether.
I'm just a wanker compared to Caniff. Can't you see?

...on a day of dark despair.
I need a theme!
A bigger subject!
The world needs one!

One pantheon steps down and lets another step up.
Caspar, come and take these old comics off me

Nothing's fixed.
They're even worse wankers than me compared to Caniff, Tad, Clare Briggs..
Who?

Immortality isn't forever.
If the greats are already forgotten, what chance do any of us have?

It's your duty to your art, you argue, to go out there and have a few global adventures.

You edit your files, your cuttings, your 'power battery', down to what will fit in this old trunk and leave the rest with friends. You give away your two jackets. Won't be needing them now.

They'll all be seeing you off. Danny Greys there.

And your brother, Mark, will lug you to the exit gate, while your Mother sheds a tear.

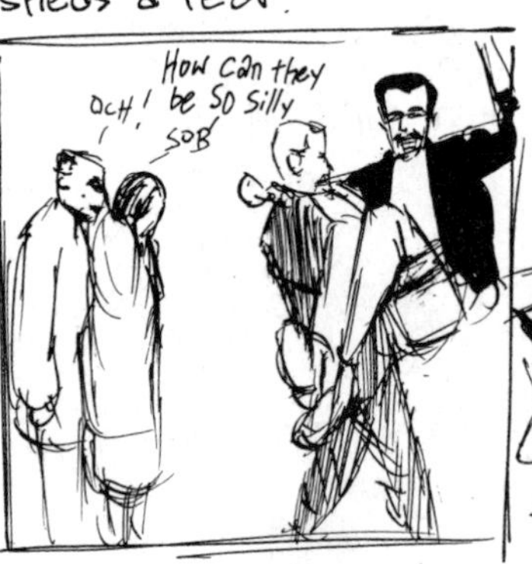

OCH!
How can they be so silly
SOB

Then you're on the plane and there's no more thinking about it.

You'll be living for a year rent-free on a tropical beach in Annie's parents' house in *Little Italy*, mailing off your comic-book falsities.

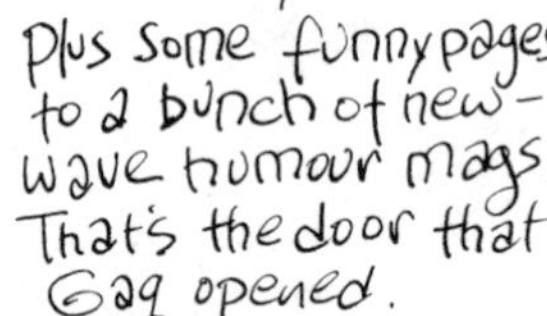

Plus some 'funny pages' to a bunch of new-wave humour mags. That's the door that Gag opened.

Until this whole end of the market will suffer what it is bound to suffer when tens of thousands of collectors speculate wildly on amateur enthusiasm.

You're broke and you've exiled yourself, you idiot.

You go on the road to find a solution to your empty bank account. The road responds like everything else.

Every now and then somebody hitches a lift and gets murdered and the whole practice gets a bad name

But truck drivers will go out of their way to drop you somewhere useful, Alec MacGarry, and you'll always try to leave them with some bit of wisdom they won't get elsewhere.

The cool night air stimulates a sense of infinity, of endless possibility.

Sci-fi dimension upon dimension where your story will work out differently every time

You spend two weeks living in a dingy closet where you'll add the final touches to your book.

The pause will give you a pocket of lucidity.

You watch the prozzies arguing across the road, under the stars. They see it not.

After three annual showings, the fourth and final part of your graphic novel will have already failed to appear.

The *Man at the Crossroads* will hawk the complete thing around the book publishers but with no success, and this in the YEAR of the graphic novel

You'll get him to send you back the few hundred £ pounds £ with which you had earlier shored up the project at a time when the Escape boys needed backing more than anything.

The cash will be as though from heaven. Here's to Bacchus.

It will dawn on you that you have apparently made your third and final lapse of faith in the bargain you struck with Fate.

when did it happen ?

You will imagine that you have murdered your muse.

Maybe you want too much. You'll have had a notion of an art that would be the inevitability of all that preceded it. The culmination of the comic strip.

Its last hooray before draining the glass and retiring into the night.

You only wanted to be left alone long enough to get on with it, like Frank King adding day by day to his life-sized picture of small-town America until it was fifty years long.

MILTON TOOK TEACHER SOME GRAPES BUT I'LL TAKE HER A PRETTY CATERPILLER!

© Trib News. Frank King 1926

Fifty years of little days. This is the 'Great American Novel', claims Richard Marschall a little hyperbolically

TULA IS A HONEY! THERE AREN'T MANY I'D TAKE HOME AFTER MIDNIGHT AND COME BACK WITHOUT GROUSIN'
2-28

© Trib-News. Frank King. Feb 28 1942

Oh, to be given enough time to create a significant work; A landmark; a lighthouse.

46 years old! Nina, in four more years I'll be 50!
2
15

© Trib-News. Frank King. Feb 15 1967 /w Dick Moores.

You never asked for fame or notoreity. Perhaps you didn't ask for enough.

SHOOT ME AND HAVE IT OVER!
OH, NO! WE WILL DIE IN THE CRASH— BUT FIRST I WILL AT LAST MAKE LOVE TO YOU!
TERRY
the nemo bookshelf
The Complete E.C. Segar

To create the stories that are the dialogue the world has with itself.

On the other side of the world they'll be putting out very nice volumes of the works of your heroes, and here you are with no money.

You once received this criticism:

You're living too much in your own head, MacGarry

hmn

Your files will have to do. How you live in the information in these old drawings. To be able to give that to readers! Not a million of them: a few devoted ones will suffice

But hey! To cultivate a separate life from the one happening in front of you. There's a thing to pursue.

...YOU DO UNDERSTAND, DON'T YOU, TERRY? I'VE GOT TO GO TO AUSTRALIA! I MUST KNOW!
RATES

© Tribune-New 1946. Milt Caniff.

CAN I COME IN?

I WUNDA WHO THAT STRANGER WAS THAT "MR. STORK" WON FROM?
AH-H.
HERRIMAN

© King Features - 1928 - George Herriman

An inside life, where Fate talks to you, sometimes in the charming tones of a girl singer with old Jazz bands.

when you consider
The highest bidder
can't buy the dream in your eye
You're a lucky guy

Othertimes in a naive wee voice in which all things are still possible.

Eh?

Go for it.

Conceit is no criticism here in the realm of the spirit as it is in real time where your heroes are long gone.

TERRY AND THE PIRATES

On an airfield in China, Terry Lee is still kissing Jane Allen goodbye.

© Tribune/News. Dec 29 1946 Milt Caniff.

In Gasoline Alley, Skeezix is having his midlife crisis.

All those years! And what have I accomplished? Not much!

You own a garage and we have a nice home, Skeezix!

© Trib News. Frank King Feb '67.

In a vast silent Arizona desert, a Coconino moon pours out molten silver.

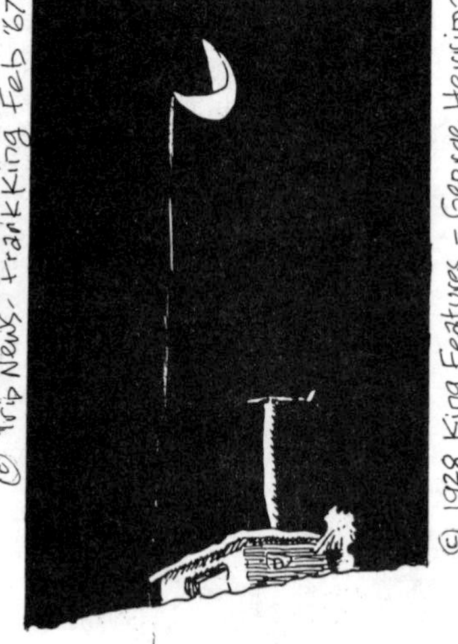

© 1928 King Features – George Herriman

It drips on Alec MacGarry, asleep at the turnpike

That's Fate taking another voice, painting a new picture in your head...

...of the road you will follow when you awake.

And follow it you will, but after this drama is done. Take your seats, ladies and gentlemen, for the final act.

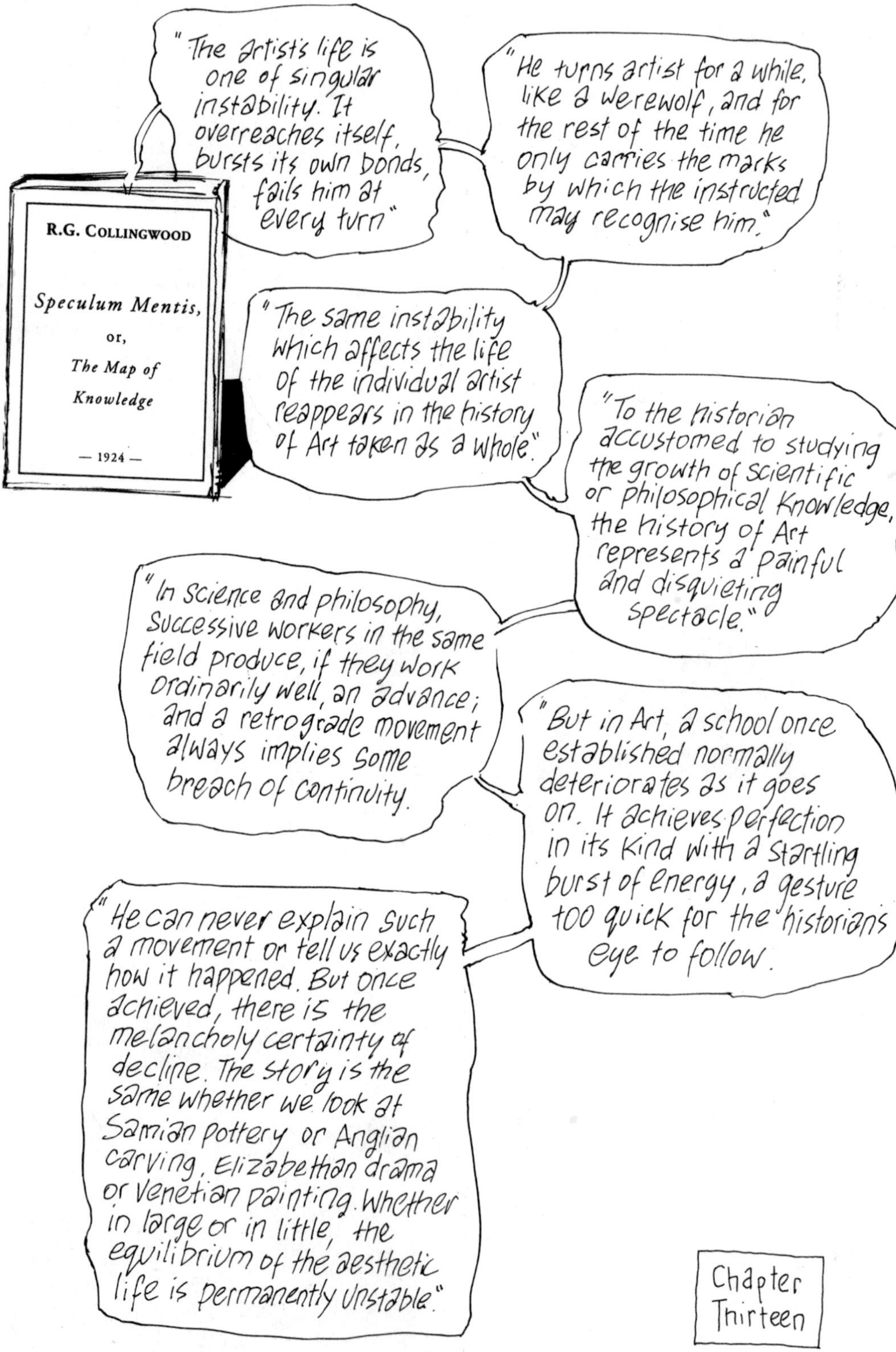

R.G. COLLINGWOOD

Speculum Mentis,

or,

The Map of Knowledge

— 1924 —

"The artist's life is one of singular instability. It overreaches itself, bursts its own bonds, fails him at every turn"

"He turns artist for a while, like a werewolf, and for the rest of the time he only carries the marks by which the instructed may recognise him."

"The same instability which affects the life of the individual artist reappears in the history of Art taken as a whole."

"To the historian accustomed to studying the growth of scientific or philosophical knowledge, the history of Art represents a painful and disquieting spectacle."

"In science and philosophy, successive workers in the same field produce, if they work ordinarily well, an advance; and a retrograde movement always implies some breach of continuity.

"But in Art, a school once established normally deteriorates as it goes on. It achieves perfection in its kind with a startling burst of energy, a gesture too quick for the historians eye to follow.

"He can never explain such a movement or tell us exactly how it happened. But once achieved, there is the melancholy certainty of decline. The story is the same whether we look at Samian pottery or Anglian carving, Elizabethan drama or Venetian painting. Whether in large or in little, the equilibrium of the aesthetic life is permanently unstable."

Chapter Thirteen

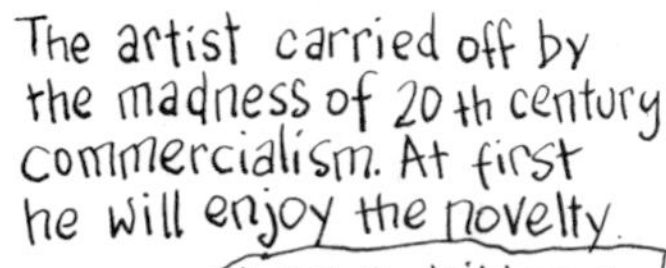

The artist carried off by the madness of 20th century commercialism. At first he will enjoy the novelty.

"We've written and drawn the comic. We've helped design the badges and approved the wristwatches."

"We've discussed the film and the role-playing game and given a nod to the t-shirt..."

"We've done the British tour and the American press interviews"

"We've done the photo session where they asked us to pose as Adam West and Burt Ward walking sideways up a wall on our bat-rope."

I don't think so

"We've signed so many books that we're thinking of swapping names just to relieve the tedium"

"and every time we see that stupid, jaundiced face with the red blood splash we get a crippling migraine"

ART: GIBBONS ©D.C.Comics 1987

There will be, much later, an article entitled: "Whatever happened to Alan Moore?" by one Nick Hasted: "In 1987 the comic book seemed the most exciting medium in existence"

"And Alan Moore had helped that happen, with *Watchmen's* clockwork precision, depth and density."

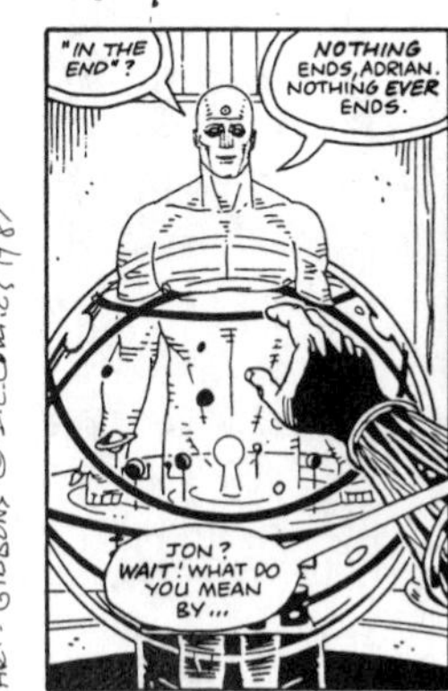

"IN THE END"?
NOTHING ENDS, ADRIAN. NOTHING EVER ENDS.
JON? WAIT! WHAT DO YOU MEAN BY...
ART: GIBBONS © D.C.Comics 1987

"When he arrived onstage at the U.K. con that year, the cheer was for a star; the comic book moment when pop and art merged."

At that same show there will be a panel discussion on the subject of *The Future of Comics*, with all the key people present, from the point of view of this thesis.
the Man at the Crossroads
Elliott (Curvapourised)
Dakin
Eisner
Big hairy Alan Moore
Spiegelmaus
Billy the Sink
new area of specialty: making the catalogues for a number of gallery exhibitions with comics links. Escape now a flash magazine
Just done a travel comic, small press
Just out with *The Dreamer*, an autobiographical subject, the artist as a young man in 1939 at the beginning of the comic book era
SO...YOU'RE VINCENT'S NEW GENIUS... HAVE A DRINK!
THANKS ...DON'T MIND IF I DO... AHEM
© Will Eisner 1986
"I've had to reinvent the alphabet for everything I do"
Graphic virtuoso.
illustrated a couple of Frank Miller books and is now about to test the boundaries of intelligibility with his own graphic novel in 4 parts, *Stray Toasters*.
© Bill Sienkiewicz . 1988
And didn't that future look quite rosy. Moore's memory of the day, however, will sound a note of despair.
"I was just held pressed up against a stairwell for almost the entire convention"
"I arrived at one panel late, the only one I was on, and for the rest of the time I was hiding in the hospitality room. I couldn't get out of the door."
The last straw may well go down as apochryphal.

Sick of it all, the big hairy one will cease appearing at conventions, except a couple of foreign ones then that's the end of it.

Furthermore, at the end of the year he will fall out irrevocably with WATCHMEN publisher DC over impending censorship impositions brought about due to the sudden public spotlight on the medium.

"They would surrender to the book-burners"

Next, he will announce his intention to self-publish, using the funds of his success to set up his independent imprint, MAD LOVE. Under this banner he will create works of a more serious nature.

We were caught on the Main Street of culture wearing our underpants outside of our suits.
MAD LOVE

It's Dave Sim of Canada that will put him up to it. Sim has his own story, which touches this one but briefly. At the centre of it is the politics of distribution in the comics market, and the balance of rewards.

CORP. CORP.

PUBLISHER

EDITOR

SURE–I'VE THOUGHT ABOUT SELF-PUBLISHING BUT IT SEEMS SO RISKY...

© 87 - Dave Sim.

He'll call together the leading creative figures to a "summit" on self-publishing, a message of empowerment which he is disseminating with holy zeal.

For about as long as an afternoon, they'll be referred to as "the gang of 12" and by this device Sim will place himself in our view...

DAVE SIM HOSTS TORONTO "SUMMIT"

Guests at the summit. Left to right: Laird, Eastman, Sim, Murphy, Totleben, Bissette, Kneeling: Zulli.

Dave Sim hosted a "summit conference" with six other comics professionals who self-publish or ar– con-sid–ring self-publishing th–

Several other items of business were announced or decided at the meeting. Sim announced that he would be

© Comics Journal '88.

... though he belongs there anyway. Having already gathered his ten years of work into four volumes, he commences a fifth, but this time with an integrated structure and meaning from the outset. This will be JAKA'S STORY which he'll collect in 1990.

© 88 - Dave Sim / Gerhard.

In assembling this 'gang', Sim will get the big name guys caught in the censorship row: Brits Moore and Gibbons, Yanks Miller and Billy the Sink and then Bissette of muck monster fame.

Then the guys in his own distribution fight, and the *Turtles* guys, which brings us to the daftest curiosity of all.

Borrowing 2000 bucks from an uncle, these two, Eastman and Laird, between '85 and '89, without finacial savvy or any particular common sense, parlay it, with an enthusiastic amateurism, into a fortune.

© Laird/Eastman '88

"We're not millionaires yet, but we may be by the end of the year."

We just wanted to not have to do stupid kitchen jobs.

Strange bedfellows, these unabashed boy hobbyists, catapulted to loony fame, and Moore, with his highflown seriousness as he announces his most ambitious work, in collaboration with virtuoso illustrator Billy the Sink.

Indeed it will be the most ambitious comic ever conceived, to be titled *The Mandelbrot Set*, until mathematician Mandelbrot will request that his name be removed.

Benoit Mandelbrot

You see, I'm having a hard enough time getting my ideas accepted without my name being the title of a comic.
I completely understand

"The vocabulary is being created now by the different people who are working, like Alan Moore and Frank Miller. We're making it up as we go along."

↑ Now they're doing rock-star photo-shoots! →

Big Numbers it will be then, using a metaphor sprung from the mysteries of fractal maths

"It's a medium that still hasn't produced its *Citizen Kane* of comics, or its *Mona Lisa* or its *Swann's Way*, but that's not to say it isn't capable."

Moore clarifies two principles of his new-found autonomy: that he will sink or swim as an independent, and that fellow independents will hang together to avoid hanging separately

Bissette will establish his own imprint, *Spiderbaby* and under this will launch a quarterly anthology entitled *TABOO*. Prolific, as ever, Moore offers his next big book for serialization in here

Suddenly you'll get a call and they'll be enlisting you to draw it. This comes completely out of the blue, though your *Pyjama Girl*, a story of murder, is the obvious connection.

For all your friendship, you will thus far have felt yourself and Moore to be in mutually exclusive camps. It comes as a shock to see that you've met somewhere in the middle.

You won't have realised you've drifted so far off your original course.

Long ago you imagined the adventure of art was Monet in his houseboat. Now it's Odysseus all at sea for ten years.

Strapped to the mast so he can't get where the action is.

WATCHMEN, with its formal complexities and its swan song of the superhero, is a novel of modern America, a work of Art even, using comic-domain archetypes the way that *Maus* does.

Now you're drawing Jack the Ripper, perennial standard of cheap horror literature, as a symbolic midwife of the twentieth century.

Around the same time, in a bold move, Gaiman and McKean land a serialized graphic novel in style magazine *The FACE*.

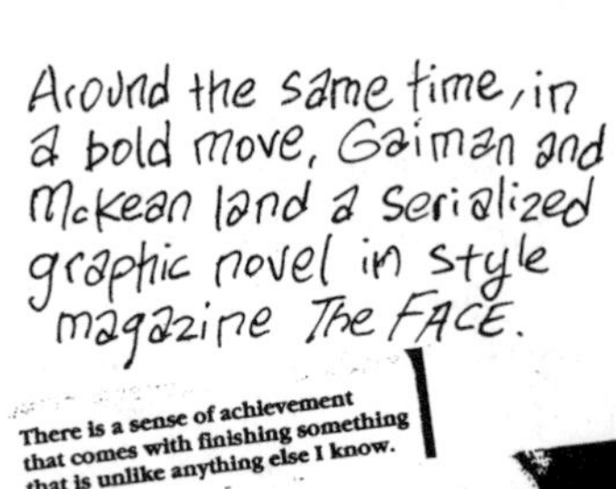

There is a sense of achievement that comes with finishing something that is unlike anything else I know.
It's about people, I suppose.

© Gaiman / McKean 1989

"It is no more acceptable to toy with the profane than with the sacred" (observes critic Rob Rodi.)

THE · COMICS JOURNAL

Signal to Noise, like *Big Numbers*, will employ a technological conceit with open graphic possibilities.

"We're still working out the vocabulary"

It'll be relaunched a year later in new colour comic mag *CRISIS*, but by then time will be running out.

© Morrison / Yeowell 1990

Following that lead, Morrison and Yeowell will launch the splendid *New Adventures of Hitler* in Scottish style mag, *CUT*. The staff object and start walking out.

© Morrison / Yeowell - 1989

It's '90 and all the promise of '88 is in danger of fizzing out, with no work of substance ready enough to follow *Maus* and *WATCHMEN* into the bigger book market. The window of opportunity is blowing shut.

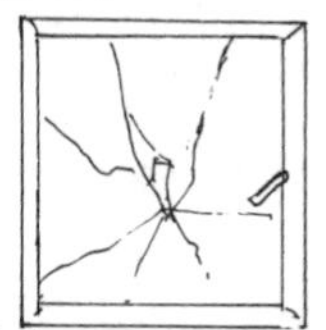

Billy the Sink turns this way and that, to show a flourish of caricature cards here,

GENERAL JORGE RAFAEL VIDELA

GENERAL FRANCISCO FRANCO

JOHN FITZGERALD KENNEDY

MARILYN MONROE

LEE HARVEY OSWALD

© Eclipse, Art: Sinkiewicz 1990

a colourful adaptation of *Moby Dick* there, and takes a bow.

-Right- so named because it is easy to kill and full of oil.

Art: Sinkiewicz

He delivers two parts of the promised twelve of *BIG NUMBERS* over a too-long wait before the project runs aground and Moore falls out with him

© Moore / Sinkiewicz 1990

The *Citizen Kane* of comics, in pieces on the cutting room floor; the *Mona Lisa*, ripped from its frame, and everybody's still working out the vocabulary.

Movie, TV, toys, etc. The *TURTLES* boys reportedly take in 50 million in the two years 90-91.

© Moore/Sienkiewicz 1991 from the legendary lost third vol.

Turtle Eastman takes his fortune and creates a publishing house called *TUNDRA*, founded upon the finest principles of artistic freedom, to be remembered as "the biggest and most absurd catastrophe in the history of comics" Groth, Comics Journal

oh that woolly mammoth.

One of his first endeavours is to take over the publishing of *BIG NUMBERS*. Billy the Sink's ex-assistant Al Columbia will draw in a continuation of Billy's style.

© Al Columbia - 1993

Let's step aside for a moment. How to be an artist, indeed! Here is the bright-eyed young hopeful just out of high school

Little wee AL
So you want to be a cartoonist I can help you.

Following the chance encounter with a photocopier rep who will have sold a machine to Stan Drake, AL gets to meet some real professionals.

Stan, I brought this young guy into town to meet you.

Billy the Sink will at this time have studio space next to Drake's. Little wee AL will have imagined these mighty ones working in 'opulent dens' and lunching on 'a sea-side deck'

© King Features. Juliet Jones by Stan Drake 1958

Oh, but they're in "tiny closets". Never mind, Little wee AL can hardly believe his luck, getting to meet his idol, Billy the Sink.

Bill. There's a guy here wants to meet you.

"Bill seemed eight feet tall, even though he was smaller than me", AL will later say.

With such ease are dreams realised; Little wee Al shows his portfolio, mostly imitations of Bill, and three weeks later he gets a call to come up to town and be Bill's assistant.

Hey, I could use someone like you

Of course, at first Al will just be sweeping and running errands, but Bill will have promised Little Wee Al a chance to work on his big new project, *Big Numbers*

"He paid me five dollars an hour. I think this was more out of kindness at first, because I was no help at all. I'd spend five hours painting a teapot.

WELL, I'M NO NEARER.
SHE DOES 'AVE MILK IN 'ER TEA STILL, DON'T SHE?
©Alan Moore-Bill Sinkiewicz '90

"But we would stay up long hours together; sometimes we'd goof around and have fun, rubber cement our lips to our noses, gossip, tell jokes"

"Bill and his girlfriend, Betty, became like an uncle and aunt to me."

© Betty: Archie comic pubs inc.

"I imitated his mannerisms, dressed like him, even wore his fancy suit-jackets into town on errands"

Bill will have started to feel uneasy about Al's imitations. He'll have seen the lad becoming him before his eyes.

"When *Big Numbers* #1 saw print I was excited to see Bill had thanked me. When #2 was released, I was irritated to see no mention of me, even though that was the one where I helped the most".

"Journalists would come and there would be photo sessions, but most of the articles on *Big Numbers* focussed on Alan Moore, barely mentioning Bill".

Billy the Sink will have been hired to illustrate a set of political 'trading cards' with a writer named Veronica, sister-in-law of the publisher of same.

© Veronica: Archie Comics Pubs.

Some people will have thought they're having an affair. Betty will have thought Al would know and grilled him over the phone while Bill's out of the studio.

"I was in no position to tell her anything and was certainly not going to betray Bill."

Little Wee Al will allege: "Betty got hold of Bill, apparently to bluff him, and told him that I had ratted him out which wasn't true."

According to Al, Billy the Sink will have admitted to Betty that he had begun an affair with Veronica. Betty then tells the publisher's brother.

Bill will have been distraught at what this revelation could mean to the trading card project.

oh fuck!

"Al will accuse: In order to salvage his professional relationship with the publisher, he threw me to the wolves. He kicked me aside like a dead cat."

We can get this thing back on track

"He continued with Veronica, wrote a check to Betty for a chunk of cash and gave me two hundred dollars severance pay."

It's at this juncture that Billy will have left *Big Numbers* in the lurch and *Tundra* approaches the novice to ask him to take over.

We can get this thing back on track

"I half expected Bill would give me his blessing," the young Al will say, "Instead he informed everyone that I was deranged".

Are you kidding? The guy's a nut!

Tundra editor Jenkins will say: "Bill told us this kid is a menace, a lunatic who's not right in the head, but we only gave him half an ear. Here was Bill, dropping the ball and complaining about somebody else's ability at the same time"

"The enormous tectonic plates of Alan Moore, Billy the Sink, Kevin Eastman and a potload of money would have ground pretty much any other young cartoonist to paste," a sensitive observer will later note.

THE·COMICS
JOURNAL

Kim Thompson, 2000.

Labouring under this betrayal, the sensitive and confused young artist will come to see his work as a "replicant abomination"

"This is a fraudulent use of my skills"

Around the world, there are kids going to their beds dreaming of being comic artists. Three of them will be in the tableau below.

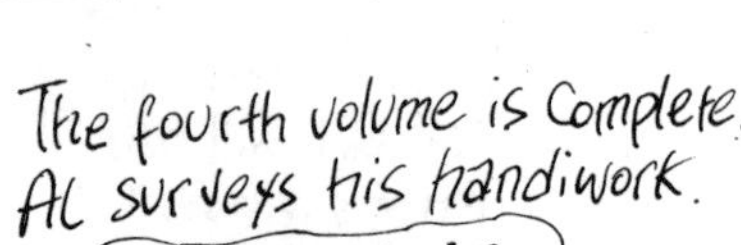

Unfair! He's stealing my thunder
You want a fuckin Sink clone - you don't want fuckin AL

But, AL, that's why we brought you in. You agreed to it!

The fourth volume is Complete.
AL surveys his handiwork.

I'll deliver it in the morning. I'll just paste over this figure
That's great AL

Paid in full for the job, Little wee AL destroys it and disappears

a small cut out figure on the floor of the studio rented for AL is all that is ever found of BIG NUMBERS #4

Big hairy Alan Moore will close the book and never speak of it again.

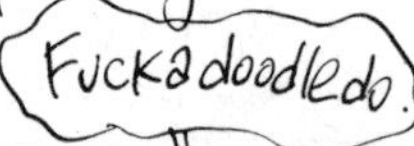

Fuckadoodledo.

Bisette will manage to get his quarterly anthology out once a year

His plans and his visions will expand inside his cranium, each pushing the other out of the way.

His visions and his plans and his plans and his visions. It'll be a stalemate. Every thing will freeze after six years.

He'll get his head clear and start over with the biography of a dinosaur. A singular idea.

He'll go visit the capable and stable Sim in Canada and work out a 15-year plan of bi-monthly issues.

He'll get four of them out in five years in this grand adventure of self-empowerment.

Time folds in on itself 5 different ways like Mexican food and maybe in a corner of the back of his head he still thinks things are getting done

The angle poise lamp burns away into the wee hours.

Alan Moore's fourth big graphic novel will take ten years to get done and Odysseus ain't home yet.

Turtle Eastman will take up the slack at year four. He's expanding his Tundra empire like crazy, funded by the Turtles.

They'll fly you into London for the opening of the U.K. division, Alec MacGarry.

The first thing they'll do is rent a big office and fill it with furniture.

They'll have a big party at the Natural History Museum, pretty girls on every arm, and the champagne flowing.

And they're getting their underpants forwarded by Fedex from hotels after leaving conventions in a squiffy cloud of intoxication.

In two years Eastman will gloriously squander fourteen million dollars on artistic follies, with genuine quality only an occasional accident.

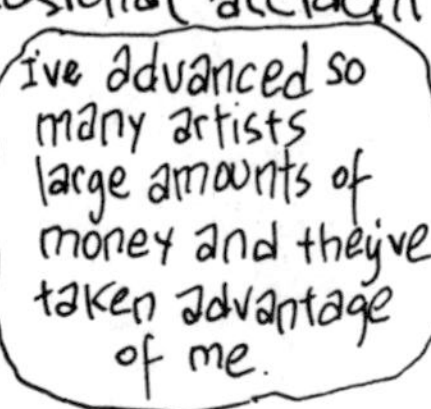

He will decide he wants out and sell the whole operation for a buck fifty.

You'll be in town again and there are not so many girlies and no champagne whatsoever.

Big hairy Alan Moore's marriage will have crashed and broken and the white suit is nowhere to be seen. The tiles are all over the place and nobody's putting them back now.

In his obituary of the comic-book great Harvey Kurtzman, Moore will recall an incident.

© E.C. Comics 1952

Halfway through what he will describe as "the lousiest week" of his life, He'll find himself at the Grenoble Comics Festival.

Written and drawn by Kurtzman

And while there, up an alp, he'll spend time with fellow guest, Kurtzman.

"Big If."

Harvey, suffering from the debilitating effects of Parkinson's disease will be bundled up warm on an already warm day, drinking cocoa.

'Graphic Novel'

It's a misnomer, of course, but then so is 'comic book'. It has been lately discarded in some circles, but it will be a thing, like the sales receipt for a shirt, that you throw out and then find you're going to need.

Chapter Fourteen

Pedants may demand a literal reading of the words. Stay away from them, Alec MacGarry. They'll want to subdivide it, as though a "novel" has a prescribed weight, into "novella" and "novelette", with a disregard for the origins of these words.

The term will embody the arrival of an idea; a serious intent will be brought into the common comic and remain as a trend through the last quarter of the twentieth century, perhaps further.

The trend will be revealed through attempts to build extended works using the mechanics of the humble comic strip.

They are probably to be numbered in thousands. Such a waste of paper is bound to make you wonder if the end result can be worth it.

Some will be bad, some dull, perhaps the worst crime a comic can commit. Some will be no more than regular comic books dressed up pretentiously.

Some will be well-meaning, some bright. Some may be good, even, and just not make my list because I'm a fallible clairvoyant.

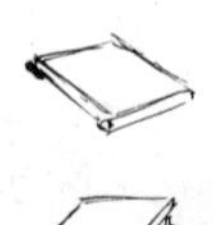

There will be around four dozen books at year 2001 whose theoretical aggregation (for in reality we cannot expect them all to like each other) will nevertheless imply a worthwhile phase in the human cultural continuum, and to be a part of such a moment is perhaps the longing at the heart of artistic ambition.

A Contract with God.
(and other tenement stories)
Will Eisner.
Oct 1977. (Baronet originally) 192 pg.
Eisner will initiate the form with this suite of stories in a small book format. The setting is the fictional Dropsie Avenue. The lead story runs to 53 pages.

A Life Force
Will Eisner
1985 (Kitchen Sink Press)
A second book by Eisner wanders too far into sci-fi, but this one will be back in the Dropsie Ave locale and extend to a good 140 pages. Will run in parts '83-'85 but not be collected till '88, after the next.

The Dreamer
To The Heart of the Storm.
Will Eisner.
1986, 1991 (Kitchen Sink Press)
With these Eisner will venture into autobiographical country. He'll be ill at ease here but you'll wish he'd gone further.

Dropsie Avenue
(the Neighbourhood)
Will Eisner
1995 (Kitchen) 168 pg.
Eisner's most ambitious construction. The history of his Bronx street Dropsie Avenue, from its 18th century origin.

Tantrum.
Jules Feiffer.
1979
Feiffer will have made extended comics before anyone (munro, etc.) Here a man starts his midlife crisis by willing himself back to 2 years old.

When the Wind Blows
Raymond Briggs
1982 (orig. Hamish Hamilton)
Briggs will have arrived via illustrating kids books. Two old folk deal with atomic holocaust

Maus.
art spiegelman
1993 (Pantheon)
In parts over 13 years from '80. (self-published for first six) first masterpiece of the form. Art and his father and his father's experience in Auschwitz. Mice, cats. Pulitzer prize winner in '92.

V for Vendetta
Alan Moore - David Lloyd.
1988 (D.C. Comics)
Will run in parts in Warrior '82-'85 and remain unfinished till '88. Dystopian vision of a fascist Britain.

Watchmen.
Alan Moore - Dave Gibbons.
1988 (D.C. Comics) 408 pg.
Collossal and intricate clock of a comic, thoroughly calculated on every level, using only the ingredients of the American Superhero comic. Parts '86-'87.

Big Numbers
Alan Moore - Bill Sinkiewicz
1990 (Mad Love)
Two parts, 80 pages, unfinished.

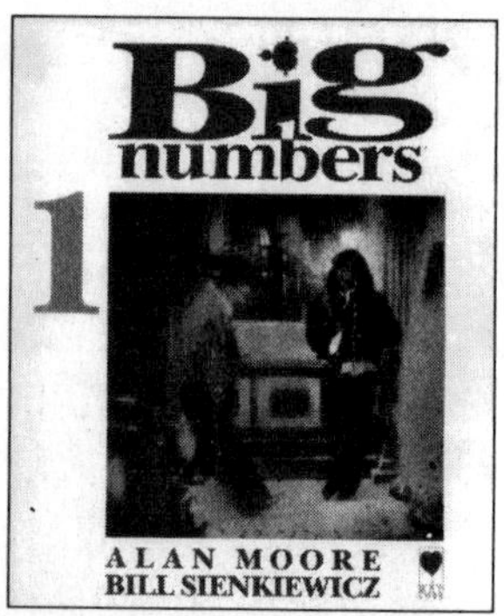

The Death of Speedy
Jaime Hernandez.
1989 (Fantagraphics)
Love and Rockets magazine by the Hernandez brothers, from '81 for fifteen years, will give us a number of great books.

Blood of Palomar
Gilbert Hernandez
1989 (Fantagraphics)
Beto's short stories of everyday life in a South American village will here expand into a full-fledged graphic novel with a cast including a serial murderer

Poison River
Gilbert Hernandez
1994 (Fantagraphics)
The lifestory of his character Luba, up to her arrival in Palomar. Structure will be complicated but repay attention.

Jaka's Story
Dave Sim - Gerhart.
1990 (Aardvark-Vanaheim)
Sim's enormous 300 issue Cerebus is true comic book ambition, but posterity will choose not to cherish all of it. This volume will stand as a moving work in its own right.

Going Home
Dave Sim - Gerhard
1999 (Aardvark-Vanaheim)
Sim's most memorable quality will be his way of incorporating caricature, a function at the very heart of the cartoon. Here, F. Scott Fitzgerald's story is subsumed into Cerebus.

Alec: The King Canute Crowd.
Eddie Campbell
1990 - (Eddie Campbell comics)
Took ten years to get it all out. 144 pages.

The New Adventures of Hitler.
Grant Morrison / Steve Yeowell.
1990 - Never collected.
Morrison's *The Mystery Play* (with Muth) and *St Swithin's Day* (with Grist) will also deserve your attention.

The Cowboy Wally Show
Kyle Baker.
1987 (originally Doubleday)
Baker will have a carefree way with structure and will perhaps want for a serious theme, but will make a couple of agreeable books.

Why I Hate Saturn.
Kyle Baker
1990 (Piranha Press - D.C.) 200 pg.
Young and vibrant in New York, like Kyle himself.

Violent Cases
Neil Gaiman · Dave McKean.
1987 (orig. Escape) 48 pg.
Subtle evocation and examination of childhood memory, with McKean using a photo-real style.

Signal to Noise
Neil Gaiman - Dave McKean.
1992 (Victor Gollancz)
A dying film director will take on one last project. Frame work of technical effects and visual sleight of hand.

Mr. Punch.
Neil Gaiman - Dave McKean.
1995 - (Victor Gollancz.) (US Vertigo)
Another dive into the psyche of childhood with its impenetrable misreadings, McKean reinvents his style here.

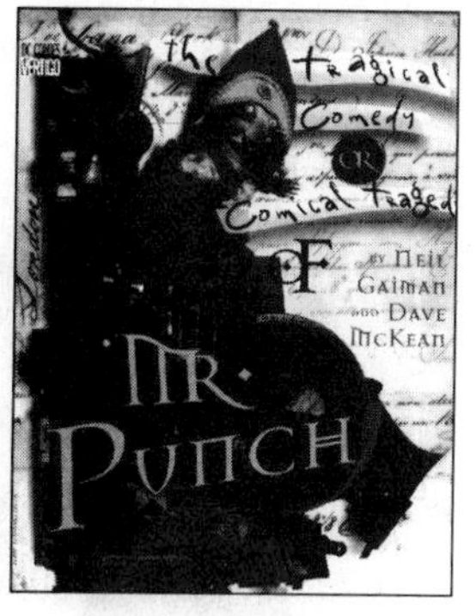

Casanova's Last Stand.
Hunt Emerson.
1993 (Knockabout Comics)
Hunt will be an engaging and unpretentious cartoonist, most of whose work will be humour of the moment. This one will endure.

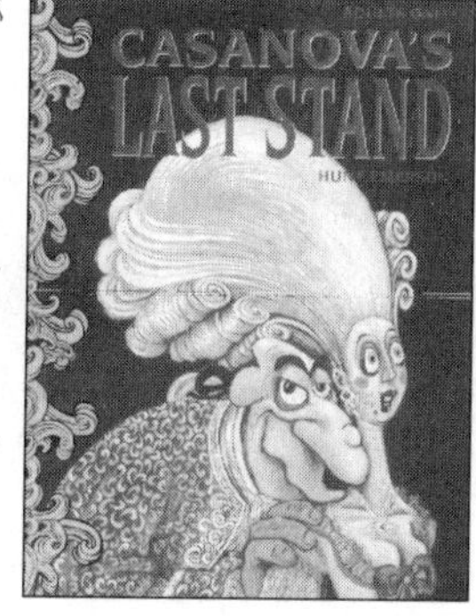

Tale of One Bad Rat.
Bryan Talbot
1995 (Dark Horse) 96 pg.
About child abuse. At the heart of it will be a loving pastiche of Beatrix Potter, famed childrens book author/illustrator.

City of Glass
Paul Auster novel, adapted by Daved Mazucchelli.
1994 (Avon Books)
At the bottom of this brilliantly sustained piece of imagination is a crime novel. The pulp style design work will add to the surreal effect.

The Playboy I Never Liked You.
Chester Brown.
1991, 1994 (Drawn and Quarterly)
Brown has a zany side, but these autobiographical books are the most sensitive comics ever made.

Stuck Rubber Baby.
Howard Cruse.
1995 (Paradox Press - DC.) 210 pg
Compelling story built around minority rights consciousness in the 1960s. At the back, Cruse will list economic tactics of four years to see the work done.

Palestine.
Joe Sacco.
1996 (Fantagraphics)
Hailed in some circles as the successor to *Maus*. Sacco will go to Palestine and record his findings in comics form.

Safe Area Gorazde.
Joe Sacco
2000 (Fantagraphics)
Will be even superior to the previous. A supreme achievement. Bosnia, from within Bosnia.

Ghost World
David Boring.
Daniel Clowes
1997, 2000 (Fantagraphics, Pantheon)
His earlier, grotesquely surreal *A Velvet Glove Cast in Iron* is also good. But these will put Clowes on the highest level.

It's a Good Life if you Don't Weaken.
Seth.
1997 (Drawn and Quarterly) 196 pg.
Seth will take himself on a real-life quest to find obscure cartoonist Kalo, revealed after publication to be a fiction. A gem.

Ethel and Ernest.
Raymond Briggs.
1998 (Jonathan Cape)
Briggs rises out of the world of childrens' books once more with this touching memoir of his parents.

Gemma Bovery.
Posy Simmonds
1999 (Jonathan Cape) 96 pg.
Well known for her weekly strips in the Guardian (U.K.) and her children's books (in comics form) Posy will have made an extended comic as early as '81. G.B. will be one of the best.

Cages
Dave McKean.
1998 (Kitchen Sink Press) 496 pg.
Example of the supreme effort needed to get a big book done. Ten parts from '90 to '96. Nearly every character an artist, musician or other creative person, all the way up to God.

Uncle Sam.
Steve Darnall - Alex Ross
1998 (Vertigo - DC) 96 pg.
Political cartoon figures and other symbols will be walking abroad in this photo-real drama.

From Hell.
Alan Moore - Eddie Campbell.
1999 (Eddie Campbell Comics)
572 pages, 10 years, 11 parts, 3 defunct publishers, one Hollywood movie.

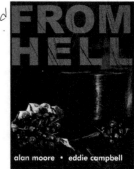

Hicksville.
Dylan Horrocks
1998 (Black Eye Press) 200 pg.
It will be a comic about the comic art process, a multi-faceted gem; narratives within other narratives, the whole delivered with great charm. Parody, parable, surreal daydream.

The Jew of New York.
Ben Katchor.
1998 (Pantheon)
From the author of weekly strip *Julius Knipl, Real Estate Photographer.* Saying what this artist's work is about would be like describing colours to blind people.

Jimmy Corrigan, the Smartest Kid on Earth.
Chris Ware.
2001 (Pantheon) (Parts: Fantagraphics)
A bleakly humourous novel of America. Three generations of Jimmy Corrigans. Their life-threads come together in the most inventively rendered family trees you will ever see.

Goodbye, Chunky Rice.
Craig Thompson
1999 (Topshelf) 128 pg.
Poetry of the cartoon form, from a new publisher.

Dear Julia.
Brian Biggs
2000 (Topshelf) 108 pg.
Boyd Solomon will believe he can fly in this little graphic novel of brittle genteel malignancy and madness.

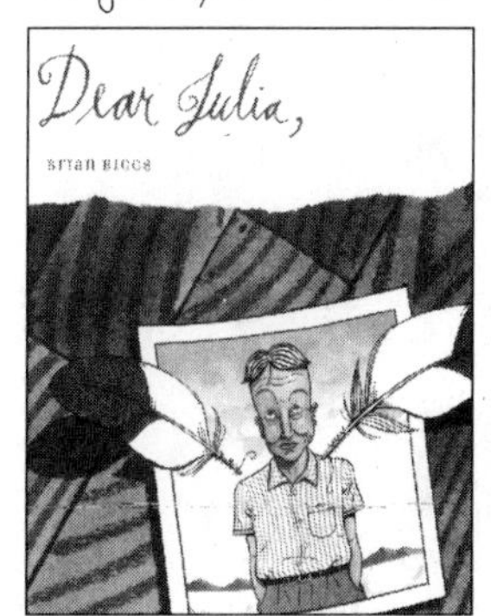

Berlin
Jason Lutes
2001 (Drawn and Quarterly)
Will be a telling examination of the heart and soul of one of the most important cities between the World Wars. Lutes' earlier book, *JAR OF FOOLS* is no slouch either

Needless to say, some of those authors listed will make shorter works superior to the long ones for which I have celebrated them. I am plotting the landmarks. May a perceptive historian map the ground between and may his book be better than some of the stupidities out there.

And you, Alec MacGarry;
you'll do well enough and
the Alec MacGarry Society,
named after a chance
remark in this book,
will keep your work
in print long after your
demise.

You can be an artist,
if that's what you
want, but you better
get started.

It's getting late.

Bugger all that hocus pocus! Just tell me what brush to use.